The Pet Detective Series

ARE SMALL FURRY RODENTS THE RIGHT PETS FOR YOU?

Can *You* Find out the Facts?

First published 2017

Copyright © Emma Milne 2017

All rights reserved. No part of this publication may be reproduced, stored in a retrieval system, or transmitted, in any form or by any means, electronic, mechanical, photocopying, recording or otherwise, without prior permission of the copyright holder.

Published by

5M Publishing Ltd,
Benchmark House, 8 Smithy Wood Drive, Sheffield, S35 1QN, UK

Tel: +44 (0) 1234 81 81 80
www.5mpublishing.com

A Catalogue record for this book is available from the British Library

ISBN 9781910455890

Book layout by Mark Paterson.
Printed by CPI, a part of Antony Rowe, UK

Illustrations by Emily Coultish and Emma Milne
Photos as indicated in the text

The Pet Detective Series

ARE SMALL FURRY RODENTS THE RIGHT PETS FOR YOU?

Can You Find out the Facts?

By

Emma Milne

BVSc MRCVS

For the Bean and the Pea.

I love you.

Contents

     Acknowledgements 6
1. The Joys of Living With Animals 7
2. Small Furry Rodents in the Wild 12
3. The Need for Fresh Water and the Right Food 20
4. The Need to be With or Without Other Animals 27
5. The Need for the Right Environment 31
6. The Need to Express Normal Behaviour 35
7. The Need to be Protected from Pain, Injury and Disease 45
8. Are Small Furry Rodents the Right Pet for Me and My Family? . 55
9. What If the Answer Is No? 63
10. Well Done, Detectives! 69

Acknowledgements

This book would not have been possible without the fantastic support, photos and help from lots of people. Thank you to the wonderful Animal Welfare Foundation and the Blue Cross. Having endorsement from such respected organisations is a great privilege. Huge thanks to Richard Saunders and the Blue Cross for keeping me accurate and for their great photos. Also many thanks to Emma Keeble (BVSc, Diploma Zoological Medicine, RCVS Recognised Specialist in Zoo and Wildlife Medicine, MRCVS), Emily Skipp, Ellie Smith, Beck Levy, Jade Hirons, Carol Boxall, Janine Campbell, Leah Marie, Sherrie, Pets at Home, Blue Cross and the PDSA for the use of their wonderful photos. Thank you to Emily Coultish for bringing my cartoon ideas to life and for putting up with my pedantry about details! I salute you all!

Chapter 1

THE JOYS OF LIVING WITH ANIMALS.

Humans and animals have shared this lovely little planet of ours for thousands of years. Over that time we've used and needed animals in all sorts of different ways. First of all we needed their bodies and we used to use all the bits we could. We ate their meat and some of the other bits too, such as kidneys and livers and hearts. We got rich nutrients out of their bones in the bit called the marrow. We used their stomachs to carry water in or to cook other bits in. Animal fat was used to make oils and candles and fuel lamps and torches. Bones and horns could be made into tools and cups and we used their skins and fur to keep us warm and dry. Even things such as a bison's tail could be made into anything from a fly swat to an ornament.

"Hey! I'm still using that!"

These days we still eat plenty of animals but we've found substitutes for some of the other bits. Over those thousands of years we started to realise that animals could be useful for other things. Cats were very good at catching mice and rats and other pests that ate our crops, so having cats around started to look like a good thing. They could do jobs for us that we found hard. Wild dogs started creeping closer to human camps to get some warmth from our fires and steal scraps of our food. But in return humans got some protection from their natural guarding instincts and we learned that if we joined them in hunting we all made a pretty good team. Horses, donkeys and camels could be tamed and could carry big loads and cover distances that man couldn't even attempt. These animals are still used all over the world today.

As more time has gone by we've stopped needing animals so much to do things for us. We have cars and tractors, we have mousetraps and food containers that can't be chewed through, we have houses with alarms and strong doors and big locks and we have farmed animals to eat so we no longer need to hunt. But the simple truth is that we found out that animals are wonderful creatures and in the time we were getting to know each other humans started to fall in love with just having animals around.

Chapter 1

THE JOYS OF LIVING WITH ANIMALS.

A dog putting its head on your lap to have his ears stroked gets some lovely affection but the human who's feeling those velvety ears and looking into those lovely brown eyes gets a lot back too. The cat stretched out on a warm rug by the fire has definitely 'landed on its feet' but the doting owner smiling in the doorway just watching the cat's tummy rise and fall with its breathing feels calm and happy without even realising it. Animals that used to just be seen as pests, such as rats, mice and hamsters, have become popular pets.

Pets make us happy. They make us feel calm and loved and wanted. Pets don't judge us or hold a grudge for days like your best friend did when you spoke to the new girl at school. They are always there and they stick with you through thick and thin. In fact, sometimes they seem a lot nicer to be around than some humans!

The Serious Bit

The last point is the bit that is so important to remember; humans don't always do the right thing for their pets. Pets don't get to decide who buys them or how they are cared for. They have to live wherever you put them and they can only have the food you give them because they can't get to food themselves. When they go to sleep, how comfortable their bed is will be totally up to you. What you have to realise is that if you want a pet, those animals are *completely* dependent on you and your family to keep them happy, healthy and safe.

It sounds like an easy thing, doesn't it? Buy a cage, or a cat bed or a dog's squeaky toy, go to the pet shop and buy a bag of food and your pet will have everything it needs. WRONG! Thousands if not millions of pets have been kept this way and, of course, with food and water most animals can survive for years but that is just not enough. A great life isn't about coping or managing or *surviving*. It's about being HAPPY! If you were locked in your bedroom with no toys or books or friends, or even your pesky sister, you'd *manage*. As long as your mum gave you bread and stew twice a day and the odd bit of fruit you'd probably live for years. But would you be happy? It doesn't sound likely does it? You'd be bored out of your mind, lonely, miserable and longing for someone to play with, even if it was just that nose-picking sister or brother that you usually avoid like a fresh dog poo and make cry in front of your friends.

Having a pet, any pet, is a serious business. It's a bit like getting married or having a tattoo: you definitely shouldn't rush into it! You need to think carefully about lots of things. What sort of house or flat do you live in? How big is your garden if you have one? What other animals, if any, have you already got?

How much money do your parents earn? Because I can tell you there is no such thing as a cheap pet. How much spare time do you *actually* have? Are you an active family or a lazy one? All these questions have to be asked and they have to be answered very *honestly*. And of course you need to ask yourself what sort of animal do you want?

I've been a bit sneaky there because actually you should *never* ask yourself what sort of animal you want. You should think about what sort of animal you can look after properly. There's a very famous song from a long time ago called *You Can't Always Get What You Want* and I'm sure your mum or dad will have said it to you hundreds of times. You probably rolled your eyes, walked off in a huff, slammed a door and shouted, 'THAT'S NOT FAIR!!' But I hate to say that your mum and dad are right, and it's especially true when it comes to keeping pets. Lots of animals get abandoned or given away because people don't ask themselves the right questions, don't find out the facts and then, most importantly, don't answer the questions honestly.

Let's be honest: you lot are masters at pestering. For as long as children, parents and pets have been around, children have pestered, parents have caved in and pets have been bought on an impulse! This means without thinking and without knowing what the animal actually needs to be happy, which usually means a very miserable pet.

But we're about to change all that, aren't we? Because now I've got the dream team on my side. You chose to find out the facts about these animals so you *could* make the right choice. And I am very proud of you for that and I am very happy. So thank you.

The EVEN MORE serious bit!

So, you are thinking it would be nice to have a pet. You're certain you are going to love it, care for it, keep it happy and, of course, NEVER get bored with looking after it and expect your mum and dad to do it. But what you need to know is that not only is that the right thing to do, but it is also now the law. Sounds serious, doesn't it, but as I said, it's a serious business. In the United Kingdom in 2006 a new law was made called the Animal Welfare Act. This law says that anyone over the age of sixteen looking after an animal has a 'duty of care' to provide for all the needs of the animal. Now, laws are always written by people who use ridiculously long words and sentences that no-one else really understands, but this law is very important to understand. A duty of care means it is the owner's responsibility to care for the animal properly, and the law means that if the owner doesn't, they could get their pet taken away and even, in rare cases, end up going to prison!

Aha, you may think, I am not sixteen so I'm fine, and you'd be right, but the duty of care then falls to your mum or dad or whoever looks after you and the pet.

Chapter 1

THE JOYS OF LIVING WITH ANIMALS.

So if you would like a small furry rodent or any pet, not only do you need to know all about them, you need to make sure the adults in the house do too. And you need to make sure they know about the law, because they might not know what they are letting themselves in for!

If you don't live in the UK you need to find out what laws there are in your country about looking after animals. But remember, even if your country doesn't have any laws like this, making sure your animals are healthy *and* happy is still simply the right thing to do.

Well, that's quite enough of all the boring serious stuff. Let's learn some things about animals! The easiest way to find out about animals is to know about the five welfare needs. These apply to all pets, and in fact all animals, so they are good things to squeeze into that brilliant brain of yours so you can always remember them whenever you think about animals.

The Need for Fresh Water and the Right Food

This is a very obvious thing to say, but you'd be surprised how many animals get given the wrong food. In fact, there was once a queen a very long time ago who wanted a zebra. I said wanted, didn't I? She definitely didn't ask herself the right questions or find out the facts, because when someone caught her one from the wild, she fed it steaks and tobacco!

Animals have evolved over a very long time to eat certain things, and if they are fed the wrong foods they can get very ill, very fat, or miss vitamins and minerals they might need more than other animals. The right food in the right amounts is essential.

The Need to Be With or Without Other Animals

Some animals live in groups and love to have company. Some animals are not very sociable at all, like me in the mornings! It's very important to know which your pet prefers. If you get it wrong, you could have serious fighting and injuries or just a very lonely and miserable pet.

The Need for the Right Environment

This is a fancy way of saying where the animal lives. It could be a hutch, a cage, a house, bedding, shelter, a stable or lots of other things, depending on the pet. It's very important that their homes are big enough, are clean, are safe and secure and the animals have freedom to move around.

The Need To Behave Naturally

Knowing what animals like to do is really important. As we said before, lots of animals will survive on food and water, but happiness, or 'mental wellbeing', is just as important as being healthy or having 'physical wellbeing'. You've probably never thought about your own behavioural needs but imagine how you would feel if you were never allowed to go to the park or play or run or see your friends. You would soon be quite unhappy. Often you find that happy pets stay healthier, just like us.

The Need to Be Protected from Pain, Injury and Disease

Animals can get ill just like us and it will be up to you and your family to keep your pet healthy as well as happy. Just like you have vaccinations, they are very important for some animals to stop them getting ill and even dying. Animals, just like lots of children, also get worms, lice, mites and other parasites. You will need to find out how to treat or prevent these and look out for signs of them.

You need to check your animals over at least once a day to make sure there are no signs of problems and take them to a vet as soon as you think something is wrong. Vet costs are not cheap. You might also have a pet you can get health insurance for, which is always a good idea.

So now you know the basic needs of all animals, it's time to concentrate on small furry rodents, or small furries for short. Rodents have been kept as pets for a while now but they still have lots of the same instincts and needs that their wild relatives have. The best way to learn what will keep your pet rodents happy and healthy is to find out what rodents in the wild are like. How do they live? What do they eat? Do they like to have others around and what makes them scared? In other words, what keeps them HAPPY? Shall we begin?

Chapter 2

SMALL FURRY RODENTS IN THE WILD.

In this book we are going to be learning all about rats, Syrian hamsters, mice, gerbils and degus. They have lots in common, as well as a few differences, but the main thing that makes them the same is that they are all rodents. The word rodent comes from a Latin word, *rodere*, which means 'to gnaw'. It's a good name for them because they all have very sharp incisor teeth like little chisels that can chew through pretty much anything! These teeth never, ever stop growing through their whole lives and they have to keep nibbling all the time to keep them worn down and healthy.

There are more than two thousand different types of rodents all over the world. In fact, rodents are so good at making the most of things and adapting that they now live on every single continent except Antarctica. The smallest one is a pygmy jerboa and is just 4.4cm long. The females only weigh about 3.75g, which is less than a sheet of A4 paper! On the other side of the scales, the biggest is the capybara and these weigh up to 66kg. That's more than me!

The pygmy jerboas are the smallest of the rodents ...

Rodents come in all shapes and sizes and are EVERYWHERE!

... and their giant relatives, capybara, are the biggest!

RODENT FACT:

Although lots of people think rabbits are rodents, they are not. They belong to a different family called lagomorphs. They have a tiny extra pair of incisor teeth just inside their big ones.

Humans and small furries haven't always been friends and their wild relatives can still be a big problem. Rats and mice especially can eat huge amounts of human crops and food and cost farmers huge sums of money. It's estimated that in 2003 in Asia, rats and mice ate enough rice to feed 200 million people! As some of these little animals are so naughty, in some places in the world it's actually illegal to have them as pets in case they escape and start breeding.

RODENT FACT:

One of the reasons rodents are so successful is that they are great at making huge numbers of babies in a short time. This means that for some rodents the males have really big testicles compared to their size. For example, the Cape ground squirrel has testicles that are about 20% of its length. If a 2m tall man was the same his testicles would be 40cm long!

Rats have had the worst reputation of any rodent in history because of something called the Black Death. This was a terrible disease that killed around 50 *million* people in the 14th century! Poor rats have been blamed for spreading the disease ever since and lots of people are still scared that pet rats spread disease. Actually, pet rats are very clean, intelligent and loving creatures. What's even more unfair is that it wasn't even the rats that spread the disease. It was the fleas on the rats that spread it, the rats just acted like school buses for them and took them where they needed to go!

Rats in history were known for spreading the plague but it was actually their fleas!

Animals never set out to be mean so we mustn't blame them for eating our crops or being a bit of a pest, they're only trying to live, just the same as us.

When humans grow and store food it's very tempting for rodents!

Chapter 2

SMALL FURRY RODENTS IN THE WILD.

So how do they like to live in the wild? One of the most important things to know about any animals to help you understand what makes them happy or scared is whether they are a prey animal or a predator. Let me explain.

Over the millions of years that there has been life on our beautiful planet, plants *and* animals have grown and evolved together in a delicate balance all linked together by the food they eat. Some animals such as degus eat plants, some, including humans and bears, eat plants and animals, and some just eat other animals. These relationships are called food chains. For rodents, one food chain might go like this:

Mouse food chain.

The mouse eats the corn and the cat eats the mouse. Prey animals are ones that are eaten and predators are the ones that eat the other animals. In the case of our food chain above, the mouse is the prey because it is eaten by the cat. The cat is the predator because it eats the mouse.

Of course, lots of animals are both predator and prey if you think about it. For example, tuna are huge fish that live in the oceans and eat smaller fish, so tuna are predators. But then a human comes along, catches the tuna and eats it in a big sandwich with some mayonnaise and sweetcorn. The tuna is the prey and the human is the predator.

Tuna food chain.

By the way, if you tried to fit the biggest tuna fish in a sandwich it would be roughly the same size *and weight* as a small car!

So now we know that rodents are prey animals and this is really important because it explains lots about the way they live, how they behave and what makes them feel happy, safe and secure. I think it's good sometimes to think about how you might feel in certain similar situations. By finding out how animals live naturally you can compare it to things in your life and it helps you to empathise with your pets. This means imagine how they might be feeling. You'll see what I mean as we go along.

That scared feeling and all the things that go with it like the racing heart are because of something your body makes called adrenaline. It's an amazing hormone, released in an instant whenever an animal (or a human) feels threatened. It's often called the fight or flight hormone. In the wild for animals to survive they either need to stand their ground and fight or, usually more sensibly, RUN AWAY!

There are still plenty of animals that could make a meal of us if we're not careful!

Imagine how you feel when you're frightened. Think about some of those scary dreams we all have where you wake up in the night and you're absolutely petrified. Something scary in your dream was chasing you and you couldn't quite get away. Your heart is pounding, your mouth is dry, you're all sweaty and it takes a few minutes to realise it was just a dream, you're safe at home and the only thing threatening you is the awful smell of foot fungus and wind wafting over from your smelly brother!

Nowadays humans don't often need to run away from a lion or a bear but adrenaline still kicks in in plenty of other scary situations; at exam time, when you have to walk past the school bully, when you're taking the all-important penalty shot that could win the game and, of course, when your mum shouts for you and uses your *middle* name. You know you're in trouble then.

Now imagine being a prey animal. Those chasing dreams aren't just dreams; they're things you have to look out for every single minute of every single day. Prey animals have various ways of avoiding being eaten depending on what sort of animal they are, where they live and also on what sort of animal is trying to eat them. Some use camouflage, some play dead while some are quick runners. Some have fearsome defences such as horns and some, like the skunk, just smell *really* bad! But lots of prey animals, including most small furries, use the form of defence that human armies use and that is strength and safety in numbers.

15

Chapter 2

SMALL FURRY RODENTS IN THE WILD.

Living in groups has lots of advantages.

Living in a group has lots of advantages. There are more eyes and ears on the lookout for danger. With more lookouts everyone gets more time to eat, play and groom. Moving as a group can confuse predators because they suddenly forget which one of you they were after in all the chaos. And, quite selfishly, any one animal in the group is less likely to be eaten the more animals there are around it. Think back to your 'adrenaline rush' at the sight of the school bully. Would you rather go past him (or her!) alone or with a group of your friends? Sometimes we all need a little moral support.

As well as being well camouflaged and living in groups, many wild rodents have more ways to avoid predators. As with lots of prey animals, they come out at dusk and dawn. Lots of predators rely on good light to see their prey. By venturing out at dusk and dawn rodents are much harder to spot. You might have heard of the word 'nocturnal' for animals that are out and about at night; well the word for animals like these rodents is 'crepuscular'.

Communication between members of a group is very important. There's not much point looking out for predators for each other if you can't tell the others when you see one. Animals communicate in different ways but lots of rodents have a wide range of squeaks and chirps and calls. Some can even make and hear ultrasonic sounds that human ears can't hear.

Prey animals in the wild are most in danger when they are babies or very young. Lots of animals that live in holes or burrows, including many rodents, have babies that are blind, have no fur and can't care for themselves at all.

Most baby rodents are born with no fur and blind.

Having eyes on the side of your head gives you all-round vision.

They tuck them away in their little nests far underground where they are as safe as possible while they grow. Some small furries live in groups that all work together to look after the babies, while others, including guinea pigs, have babies that are born like tiny adults, able to see and run and fully covered in fur.

A common difference between prey animals and predators is their eyes. Predators usually need very accurate eyesight to fix their prey and judge how far away they are. The best place to have eyes to do this is on the front of your face, pointing forwards, like humans, dogs and cats. Prey animals don't need accurate vision but they do need to see what's coming from every direction, including birds of prey from the sky. The best place to have eyes that see everywhere is on the side of your head.

Some rodents can see almost everything behind them, above them and in front of them without moving their heads. A bit like teachers! Others that spend lots of time tucked away and only venture out in dim light have quite poor eyesight. They usually have very sensitive ears, noses, whiskers and paws to make up for it though! Lots of rodents use smell to communicate too.

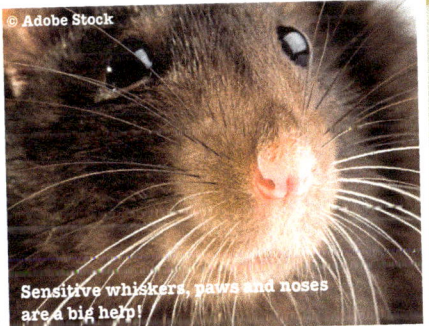
Sensitive whiskers, paws and noses are a big help!

They leave little 'signposts' of urine and other rodents can tell what species they are, if they're ready to make babies and even sometimes how important they are in their group. Degus can even see ultraviolet light and it's thought they have ultraviolet-reflecting wee so they can see urine trails as well as smell them. They also have fur on their tummies that reflects ultraviolet light. This means that if they want to tell the others to watch out but stay silent at the same time they can stand on their back legs and their shiny tummies are seen by the other degus but no one else. Clever eh?

Chapter 2

SMALL FURRY RODENTS IN THE WILD.

So, lots of small furries sleep most of the day and then they creep out at dusk or at night, they have a good look round and a listen for predators, and then what? They EAT! As you might have guessed from all the talk of how annoying rodents are when they steal our crops, the majority of them are herbivores. This means they eat plants, seeds, nuts, fruit and different vegetation. There are a few rodents that will also eat insects and other animals.

Grass, seeds and similar plants are hard to grind up and even harder to digest so animals that live on these foods have had to evolve ways to get at the goodness locked inside those tough things. Firstly, they need really good teeth.

As we said, small furries have very sharp incisor teeth like little chisels. These teeth snip through the plants like garden shears and then the food is pushed to the molar teeth at the back to be ground up. Some of these foods such as leaves don't contain many nutrients so animals living on them need to eat A LOT to get everything they need. Some seeds, nuts and grains have very hard outer cases that need to be chewed through. All that nibbling wears teeth down pretty quickly. This is why their teeth must keep on growing or they would soon disappear altogether!

RODENT FACT:

The grasshopper mouse eats insects (like grasshoppers), scorpions, poisonous centipedes, snakes and even other mice!

Now I'm going to tell you something about rodents that is going to make you very glad you're a human and not a small furry. There is something else they eat besides grass, seeds and other plants. Their own POO! That's right, the way many rodents get all the nutrients out of their tough diet is by eating it *twice*. Eating poo is called coprophagy and for many animals it's simply essential. Rodents produce soft poo called caecotrophs, which is covered in mucus a bit like snot. They eat this snotty poo straight out of their own bottom. Yum! The mucus protects the poo from all the strong acids and juices in the stomach and then when it gets further down the intestines it is digested a second time and all the vitamins, minerals and goodness get a second chance to be absorbed.

"eat up then, darling"

So now you know pretty much everything there is to know about small furries in the wild, we better get down to the tricky business of keeping them as happy, healthy pets. First, let's look at the absolute essentials; water and food.

Chapter 3

THE NEED FOR FRESH WATER AND THE RIGHT FOOD.

We've already said that a great life is what we should try to give all our pets and the best start to that is to get the basic survival stuff exactly right from the very start. The top three things needed for life are air, water and food. Animals, including humans, can't live without these things and when it comes to food, getting the right diet and feeding the right *amounts* of food will get your small furries off to a brilliant start for a healthy and happy life.

Let's tackle the easy part first. Water. Water is absolutely essential for every living thing on Earth. For animals such as humans and small furries, after the need for air, water is the most important thing. If animals can't get to enough water they can get very ill and die really quickly. In general, the smaller the animal the more quickly they get dehydrated and ill, so you need to be very watchful of your small furries. Water is the only thing they will need to have to drink. Depending on the food you give them, they will also get some water in their food, say for instance in some juicy leaves or vegetables, but it's essential they have access to plenty of fresh water all the time as well. Just like us, they will need to drink more during warm weather compared to cold weather, and also if they've been very active, climbing, burrowing, exploring and playing.

Lots of you will have seen the water bottles that most small animals have attached to the sides of their cages. These are great but it's very important that you check that they are working at least twice a day. Sometimes the little balls that let the water flow out of the nozzles can get stuck. If this happens it might look like your small furries have plenty of clean water but they actually can't get to it! This would be very frustrating for them but is also very dangerous because water is so vital for life.

When you check the bottles make sure the water is clean and there is plenty available. You still need to change the water in the bottles once a day even if it looks clean because it can get stale or algae can start growing in it, which can make your small furries poorly.

Wild animals spend lots of time searching for food.

© Adobe Stock

Lots of the food rodents eat is either hard to digest or hard to actually get into!

© Adobe Stock

So, first we need air, then water and then, of course, we need food. Bodies are amazing machines and make any computer or machine that humans have built look like the most ridiculously rubbish toy imaginable. Like all machines, bodies need energy to make them work. As our bodies are so spectacularly clever they can also fix themselves and replace their own parts; instead of plastic and metal bits or replacement batteries they need vitamins and minerals, fibre, proteins, fats and carbohydrates. All animals get these from their food and over the millions of years that animals have been on the planet they have evolved different ways to get all the things they need from their foods. Small furries need to explore to find food and work hard to get it. Then they need to chew it really well and they eat it twice to make sure they get every scrap of goodness out of it by eating their own poo.

Before we look at what our different small furries eat, there is one thing we must say first and that is that the amount of food you give your pets is just as important as getting the diet right. Lots and lots of humans give their pets more food than they need because it makes us feel kind and we don't like the thought of animals being hungry. The trouble is that all animals, (including us!) have evolved over millions of years in a perfect balance with nature. Animals in the wild work hard for their food and the supply of food is never guaranteed.

21

Chapter 3

THE NEED FOR FRESH WATER AND THE RIGHT FOOD.

Small furries' bodies have evolved to be experts at getting every scrap of goodness out of their food. So when humans come along and give them an easy supply of as much food as they can eat they can easily get way too fat. Being too fat, or obesity as it is called, is a real problem for animals and humans alike. You don't find fat animals in nature. Some animals will build up stores of fat to keep them warm and give them energy through the winter but you will never find a truly fat animal in the wild. Being too fat can give lots of animals diseases and the extra weight puts strains on joints and bones and gives the heart too much work to do. You can imagine that a fat prey animal might struggle to get away from a predator and wouldn't live long enough to have fat babies. This really is survival of the fittest!

Being overweight can also make it very hard to keep clean. Lots of animals need to groom themselves to stay clean and keep their fur and skin healthy. Being too fat makes this really hard and for small furries especially this is a big problem. We'll look at these problems more in Chapter 7 but for now all we need to know is that the right diet and the right *amount* of food is really important.

So now we know that feeding amounts is very important it's time to say that so is the *right* food. Small animals need to eat much more often than bigger animals because they use lots more energy for their size. This means we usually try to make sure our small furry pets have food available all the time. I'm sure you can guess from what we just said about being too fat, that if we give them food full of energy all the time they will soon pile on the weight.

"Well, this is going to be easy!"

Rodents do have lots in common but we need to remember they come from very different places in the world, they live in different environments with different foods on offer and they are different species of animals. So there might be things they can all eat but you must never assume that food for one animal is safe for another. For instance did you know that raisins and grapes that we love to eat can easily kill your pet dog?! In fact, grapes make a lot of animals poorly so are best kept for us humans. So let's look at our small furries and see what they like to eat and what keeps them healthy.

Degus live in groups and eat lots of grass and leafy plants. They are herbivores.

Degus

Degus come from Chile in South America, live in burrows and they love to dig. Sometimes they are cheeky and move into other animals' burrows to save themselves some time and effort! They are strict herbivores, which means they only eat plants. They're actually related to guinea pigs and chinchillas and they mostly eat grass, leaves and other leafy plants. They will occasionally eat seeds but most of their time is spent grazing.

Animals such as this, the same as guinea pigs, really need to have lots of what's called long fibre in their diets, including grass, leaves and hay. You can pick grass for your pet degus but never give them cuttings from a lawnmower because these can go off very quickly and make them ill. Make sure they have good quality, dust-free hay to eat all the time.

This is really important for keeping their teeth and their intestines healthy as well as keeping them slim.

All small furries get offered a little bit of dry food but degus are special when it comes to this. Degus can't tolerate virtually any sugar in their diet, even the natural sugar in fruit, and are very prone to a disease called diabetes. For this reason, it's very important that you only give them either special degu dry food or a mixture of guinea pig and chinchilla pellets. You also need to check the packet if you use guinea pig or chinchilla food to make sure there are no sweet additives such as molasses or honey. Go to a reputable pet shop where the staff are well trained, or if you are in any doubt ask your vet if the food you have is OK.

Never give degus unlimited pellets or they might not eat enough fibre and hay. They only need about half an eggcup full each a day. As occasional treats, you can also offer them leafy vegetables, dandelions, broccoli or green beans. If you buy treat sticks from a pet shop you need to be sure again that they are safe to give to degus and have no added sugary things.

Once a day, maybe when you're checking the water bottle, take out any uneaten fresh food so that it doesn't go bad. Like many rodents, degus like to hoard food so they always have some around, so you might need to root about a bit to make sure you find it all!

Pet degus need to have hay to eat all the time.

Chapter 3

THE NEED FOR FRESH WATER AND THE RIGHT FOOD.

Muesli-style mixes let animals pick their favourite bits so …

Gerbils

Gerbils eat plants and animals. They are omnivores.

Gerbils come from really dry grasslands and desert areas in Africa, India and Asia. They are also known as 'desert rats'. As they live in a dry climate they are very good at not wasting water and don't urinate (wee) as much as some other rodents. This makes them popular with some people who don't like mess and the smell of wee!

In the wild, gerbils are omnivores, like humans. This means they eat plants and animals and in the wild they will eat insects and grubs if they get the chance. Their plant diet is mostly seeds and grains and grasses.

For your pet gerbil, the easiest thing to do is offer them a gerbil food from a good pet shop. If you ever have the choice of a pellet food instead of a mix you should get pellets. This stops your pets from picking out all their favourite bits and missing some essential bits such as vitamins and minerals. Imagine if someone gave you a pick 'n' mix that had sweets, fruit and cabbage in it. I'm guessing the cabbage would be the last to get eaten! Gerbils, like children, also tend to just pick out their favourite bits and can quickly get too fat or have an unbalanced diet. Having all the foods in a pellet stops this from happening. If you do feed a mix, talk to the pet shop and make sure the mix mimics what gerbils would eat in the wild as much as possible. Avoid ones with lots of sunflower seeds that are too high in energy.

Fresh fruit and vegetables, such as apples, carrots and broccoli, are good treats. Vegetables can be given more often than fruits, which are more fattening and higher in sugar. Only give about a teaspoon of fresh stuff a day. Once every week or two, a few pumpkin seeds make lovely treats too. As gerbils are omnivores you can also occasionally give them mealworms or a kibble of dry dog food for a bit of extra protein.

… it's always better to use pellets if you can get them for your pet.

Gerbils also love to hoard food. As we've said about animals in the wild, many of them don't know where their next meal is coming from. Gerbils will take food and stash it away in their tunnels. In the wild they can put up to a kilo and a half in one place. That's a lot of dinners for a small animal! You should take out hoarded fresh food every day in case it starts to rot. If you find you're throwing lots away, reduce how much you give them.

Hamsters

Wild hamsters are found in Europe, Asia and the Middle East. One of their most striking features is their ENORMOUS cheek pouches. Just as it sounds, they are pouches inside their mouths that stretch right back as far as their shoulder blades. If the food bowl is the supermarket, their pouches are the shopping bags for taking it all home!

Hamsters are omnivores too.

Watching hamsters load their pouches is incredible and makes their head look three times the size it actually is.

Watching them empty their pouches is equally as fascinating! They are the kings and queens of hoarding and their name actually comes from the German word *hamstern*, which means 'to hoard'.

Hamsters can fit HUGE amounts of food in their amazing cheek pouches.

HAMSTER POUCH FACTS:

Some mother hamsters put their babies in their cheek pouches to carry them away from danger. Syrian hamsters can fit *half* their body weight in their pouches. Hamsters hate to swim but if forced to they can fill their cheek pouches with air and float!

Hamsters and gerbils have very similar diets. In the wild hamsters eat seeds, grains, plant roots and leaves. They too are omnivores and will enjoy the odd insect as well as earthworms and snails. Offer them a commercial hamster food, pelleted if possible. The same extras that gerbils can have can be given to hamsters, including the odd bit of dog kibble. You can also offer occasional hard-boiled egg or mealworms.

Don't forget to take out uneaten fresh food once a day to stop it going rotten.

Chapter 3

THE NEED FOR FRESH WATER AND THE RIGHT FOOD.

You can buy treat sticks from a pet shop ...

Mice and rats

You may not know it but rats are actually in a group of animals called true mice so they have lots in common with mice. Mice and rats are quite similar in their dietary needs as well. In the wild they eat a variety of grains, seeds and fruits. They are also omnivores like hamsters and gerbils and will eat insects, grubs and other small animals. Just as we said with all the others, buy food that is designed for the animal you have.

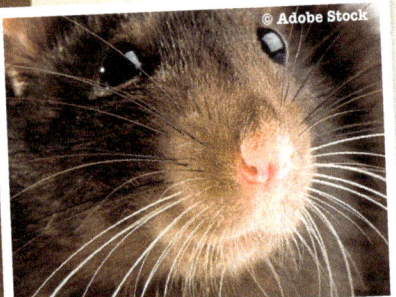

Rats and mice have similar wild diets and are omnivores.

It's particularly important that rats have pelleted food as they are very prone to selective feeding and getting too fat. You can feed rats' pelleted food to mice as well.

Mice and rats will love extras for variety such as fresh fruit, vegetables and dog kibbles, and you can even cook them little bits of chicken, egg or offer them mealworms.

If you do offer meat or eggs don't leave it uneaten for more than a couple of hours or it will start to go off. As we said with the others, take out all uneaten fresh food once a day.

I've only mentioned a few foods that make nice treats or that might be dangerous because the list is endless. Later on in your fact-finding you'll be doing some more research to find which foods are safe and which are not for these animals. If you're ever in doubt ask your vet or stick to pre-made diets until you are sure.

... or make your own fruit and veg kebabs.

You might be surprised to find out that a bowl is not the only way for you to give your small furries their food. Lots of these animals throw everything out of their bowl anyway, or take it away to hide it. Animals in the wild spend hours and hours foraging and exploring for food. There are lots of ways to make eating more interesting and keep your small furries busy. This is part of what we call environmental enrichment. It's a bit like you having posters on your wall, books to read or a TV in your room rather than a blank, white box for a bedroom. In the next few chapters we'll look at the type of 'environment' that keeps small furries happy and healthy as well as how we can 'enrich' it or make it even better.

Chapter 4

THE NEED TO BE WITH OR WITHOUT OTHER ANIMALS.

Most rodents love to live with friends and family.

All the needs of animals are important but for many animals this is probably the *most* important one for being happy, so we need to get it right. This is probably the need that humans have messed up the most over all the time we've kept animals as pets. For hundreds of years we've kept rabbits and guinea pigs on their own, rabbits *with* guinea pigs, left dogs alone for hours while we're out and got used to the 'crazy cat ladies' who have dozens of cats in a tiny house. As you may have guessed, ALL THIS IS WRONG!

If you're shocked about rabbits, guinea pigs, dogs and cats then you had better get those Pet Detectives books next but for now we must focus those brilliant brains of yours on rodents.

This is where we do need to look at our rodents in two separate sections because of one very big difference. Let's do what we should always do and think back to our wild small furries and how they like to live without humans.

Rats, mice, degus and gerbils

Like many prey animals, all these small furries are social animals. The sizes might vary but in general they live in close groups of very good friends and family. They feel safest when there are other small furries of the same species around. Think back to how they communicate and work together. If there is more than one of them they have extra eyes and ears to look out for predators. If they know someone else is on watch they can relax a little and explore and feel secure. This means they can get plenty to eat, keep their teeth and intestines healthy and stay safe all at the same time.

Not only are they prey animals, needing numbers to feel safe, they actually really like to have company. They are sociable animals. They like to play together, which for pet rodents means they will stay fitter and slimmer. They can run and chase around, especially in that brilliant environment you are going to make for them. Life should be fun for them.

Social animals love to snuggle up. It not only makes them feel safe and happy but especially in cold weather, it keeps them warm. Rodents are small animals and small animals lose heat more quickly than big animals. This is because they have a big body surface compared to their size. By snuggling together they can share warmth and slow down the loss of heat from their little bodies.

Chapter 4

THE NEED TO BE WITH OR WITHOUT OTHER ANIMALS.

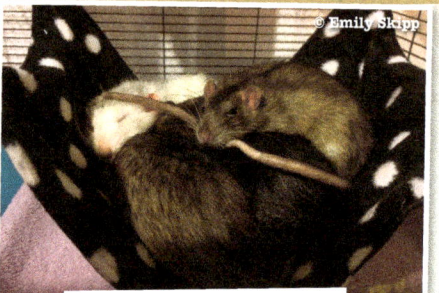

Snuggling up keeps everyone warm and happy.

They also groom each other. They can do some of it for themselves but, like all of us, they have places that are difficult to reach. You can imagine that if you only have your tongue and your paws to wash with, having a friend to help is always going to make life easier. Grooming each other helps keep their fur in tiptop condition but is also an important part of life. It helps them form relationships, bond with each other and keep the group tightly knitted together.

Although some people don't seem very friendly, we are a social species too, which means it should be easy for us to empathise with our sociable pets. Empathy is when you can imagine how a person or an animal would feel in a similar situation. For example, if you saw a dog that had been starved you could empathise because you know what it feels like to be hungry.

If you saw a cat being chased by a dog you could empathise with the cat because you know what it feels like to feel frightened. Remember when you had to imagine walking past the school bully? Social creatures feel happiest and safest when they are not alone.

Imagine how you would feel if you were never allowed to see your friends, your family or even have another single human being to talk to. You wouldn't have anyone to tell your funny stories to, you would have no one to play with and you would be extremely bored and really lonely. In fact, when humans are left completely on their own they actually go totally mad very quickly. Social animals that are left alone, sometimes even only for a little while, can have very sad lives. These small furries are just the same. So now you can see why it's so important for social animals to have company. And just as important is that they need company from the same species.

Imagine if someone thought you were lonely living in your bedroom with no humans to talk to so they put a donkey in there with you. You can't understand each other, can't communicate, have totally different diets and one of you could definitely get badly injured. This is what happens if you keep different animals together, so make sure they have the right company too!

Having friends means you can explore and have more fun!

Now, if you're going to be excellent pet owners and make sure your small furries have friends there's something very important we need to remember from Chapter 2; rodents are VERY good at having babies. In fact, lots of rodents can get pregnant the very next day after they've given birth! To be a responsible pet owner we need to avoid unwanted babies that might not get homes, so with all these small furries the easiest thing to do is keep them in pairs or groups of the same sex. This means girls together or boys together. It can sometimes be hard to introduce new animals to each other once they are adults because in the wild they all grow up together. This means it's easiest to get them as pairs or groups from the same litter or having grown up together from babies. You also need to be sure that the pet shop or the breeder has definitely worked out which are the boys and which are the girls or you could end up with some unexpected babies! You sometimes find with mice that the males fight more, so sticking to pairs or groups of females is best.

Syrian hamsters

Syrian hamsters are the exact opposite

Some animals are different and don't like company.

when it comes to being sociable and are a good example of why you can't assume all animals (or even all rodents!) are the same. Syrian hamsters are solitary creatures in the wild. They are very territorial. This means they want to keep their territory or their living area just for themselves. They guard the food and water and bedding and they are like toddlers because they hate to share! This means that if another hamster comes along they will fight really hard to get them to go away. The new hamster is territorial too and they will want to take over the area and all the nice things. Hamsters can badly injure or even kill each other if you try and keep them together, so they are actually much better off and much happier if you keep them on their own.

Chapter 4

THE NEED TO BE WITH OR WITHOUT OTHER ANIMALS.

Take care!
Some of the other dwarf species of hamsters are social and some aren't, while some vary depending on whether they are females or males; which all gets very confusing! Dwarf hamsters are tiny and can be very difficult to handle. I think Syrian hamsters are more suitable as pets, which is why I've concentrated on them for this book. If you do consider one of the other types, do your research because you definitely don't want to get it wrong.

It can be difficult for social animals such as humans to understand how an animal can be happy on its own but that is why finding out all the facts before you get a pet makes you a much better owner.

You might be thinking that at the end of the last chapter I was going to talk about environment and enrichment and then I keep forgetting. I haven't forgotten at all. For social animals, keeping them in pairs or more is the best way to enrich their environment there is! They can play, chase, watch out for each other, keep warm and groom.

For animals that are anti-social we can make sure they don't have to feel worried about sharing their most precious things.

What we're actually saying is that they can behave *naturally*. And this leads us on to the next two needs; the need for the right environment and the need to behave naturally. These things are closely linked because the environment needs to be good enough and big enough to let them do all the things they love!

Yay, let's find out where we're going to live!

Chapter 5

THE NEED FOR THE RIGHT ENVIRONMENT.

Wait. You mean I can't just live in your house?!

Just as we said in the last chapter about animals needing company or loving to be on their own, humans have also messed this up too! We are getting better but I'm hoping you are going to be gold star winners when it comes to this. Humans have a bad habit of thinking things like, 'Ah, gerbils are cute, aren't they? I think I'll have one of those.' Then they go to a shop, buy a small cage, put a gerbil in it and hey presto, one happy human and one very miserable gerbil! Humans like pets that are easy and convenient but the trouble is that the only time pets are easy and convenient is when they are not being looked after properly. Just because a gerbil can't complain or tell us what it would prefer doesn't mean it isn't suffering. Of course, you can keep a gerbil or any small furry alive like this for a couple of years but it definitely wouldn't be happy.

I know I keep saying it but to have happy pets we need to empathise and we need to think about how they live in the wild. Anyone can keep an animal alive but it's only a rare owner that has truly happy pets! Did you know that hamsters can cover up to *five miles* in one night of exploring? They're not going to be happy sitting in a tiny plastic box for two years are they?

The thing I want you to remember from this chapter is that when it comes to the right environment:

SIZE MATTERS!!!

Now there are plenty of times in your life that you will hear that size is not important but when it comes to small furry cages and enclosures it definitely does. When I was doing the research for this book do you know what surprised me? I couldn't find anyone who agreed about how big cages should be or what the minimum sizes should be. I looked in vet books, and on welfare websites, charity websites and specialist rodent websites. That isn't very helpful is it? So what I've decided is that I'm going to give you some idea of general minimums but I really want you to try to buy the biggest, most gigantic, elaborate ones you can, especially once we've looked at the things that these animals love to do in the next chapter.

Chapter 5

THE NEED FOR THE RIGHT ENVIRONMENT.

Rats and degus

© Pets at Home

Rats and degus need huge, sturdy, wire cages with lots of levels.

Rats and degus are the biggest of the small furries we are learning about and I think they deserve similar-sized cages. They both love climbing and exploring and need large, tall cages with lots of levels. You need to make sure the cage is suitable for them and the bars are close enough together so they can't squeeze through. You can't use a wooden enclosure because it's too hard to clean properly and you can't use a plastic cage because they will eat their way out of it! Get a sturdy metal cage with solid shelves and a solid floor. Wire floors are horrible for their feet and can cause painful, infected sores called bumblefoot.

- Minimum size for two rats or degus: 70cm × 100cm base, 130cm tall. You might be OK with a slightly smaller base if the cage you find is taller. For more than two animals you'll need to go even bigger.

Even these lovely big cages won't be enough for 24/7 and both rats and degus need at least an hour out of their cages every day to play and exercise in a bigger area. Remember, they can chew through pretty much anything so not only can they damage stuff when you let them out but they can injure themselves as well. You'll need to make sure there are no cables or wires they can chew and no house plants that might be toxic if they ate them. They can get into tiny places as well, so you need to be sure you'll be able to get them back again!

© Ellie Smith

You can build a play pen ...

© Emily Skipp

... or you can let them explore the house ...

© Carol Boxall

... under close supervision!

Mice and hamsters

Mice and Syrian hamsters have similar needs when it comes to cages. Try to get a wire cage with a solid plastic or metal bottom. The bars will need to be very close together to stop them escaping so make sure the one you get is suitable for these animals. Lots of shops sell plastic or glass enclosures for mice and hamsters but they can have very poor airflow that can make the animals poorly. Cages that are part plastic and part wire are fine as long as the wire sections are enough of the whole design to allow air to flow through the cage. If you buy cages with plastic tunnels on them make sure they will be easy to clean and that the rest of the cage is well ventilated. Get the biggest cage you can find with small enough bars for hamsters and mice. Don't worry if the cage doesn't have any tunnels on it because in the next chapter we're going to look at all the things you can do to make these lovely big cages like the best play parks in the world!

© Pets at Home

Lots of mice and hamster cages are tiny so go big. Gerbil cages like this one are great for them too.

Some people devote a whole spare room to this or you could section off part of a room. You'll need to supervise, though, because all rodents are brilliant at escaping! If you've got a great rodent-proof room then why not let them have the whole thing all the time? It might seem excessive but they'd be happier with the space and the freedom to go where they choose any time.

As you might have guessed, lots of people don't realise just how much room these not-so-small small furries need. If you were thinking you had a little bit of room in the corner of the living room that you could pop a couple of degus or rats in, you might need to think again.

- Minimum cage size for two mice or one hamster: 60cm × 50cm base, 50cm tall. Again, the dimensions don't have to be exactly the same, for instance a 75cm × 40cm base would still give the same floor space. As always, the bigger the better.

Chapter 5

THE NEED FOR THE RIGHT ENVIRONMENT.

Gerbils

Gerbils need a nice deep bottom!

Gerbils are a little bit different from the rest when it comes to environment because they LOVE to dig burrows. We'll be looking at all the animals' behavioural needs in the next chapter but for now you need to know that a totally wire cage is no good for your gerbils. You're going to need about 30cm of peat or soil in there for them to dig in and make tunnels, so you need at least this depth of solid glass or transparent plastic otherwise you're going to end up with peat all over your bedroom, disappointed gerbils and very unhappy parents! Most good pet shops will have 'gerbilariums'. These will have a lovely deep base to fill with tunnelling material and the best ones will have a big wire enclosure on top as well so that the gerbils can come out, explore, eat, drink and play.

- Minimum gerbilarium size for two gerbils: 75cm × 40cm (or 60cm × 50cm) base. It must be at least 50cm high so that your gerbils have plenty of room above ground to have fun.

Whatever small furries you have, there are some things that are important for all of them when it comes to their environment. You need to think very carefully about where you put them. They need to be out of direct sunlight and out of draughty areas. You have to remember that they can't escape their cages so if they are in a roasting hot conservatory or a draughty utility room they won't be able to stay at a comfortable temperature and could get very ill or even die. A temperature of around 18-20 degrees Celsius is ideal and this should be as constant as possible.

For animals such as rats, mice and hamsters, soft lighting is best because they are used to being out and about in low light. From your point of view, it's also good to remember that all these animals except degus are crepuscular or nocturnal. This means they are going to be madly scurrying around when you are trying to sleep! There are lots of children constantly woken up by the rattling of an exercise wheel. You might want to put your pets somewhere they won't be too disturbed by the hustle and bustle of the house and you won't be disturbed by them. It's also good to remember that they are prey animals and they will be very frightened by other pets such as cats and dogs, so keep them well away from each other.

So now we have their basic environment sorted out, it's time to let your imagination go wild. It's time to enrich their cages and their lives and make them super HAPPY!

Yippee! Time to have some FUN!

Chapter 6

THE NEED TO EXPRESS NORMAL BEHAVIOUR.

© Blue Cross
Did someone say 'FUN'?!

Have you ever had an itch in a place you couldn't reach? Right in between your shoulder blades, for example. You bend your arm right the way up your back but the tip of your thumb stops about a centimetre short of the itchy spot. Ooooohh, it drives you mad doesn't it? You try and ignore it but the more you try the more you keep thinking about it until you can't think about anything else. Eventually your mum finds you crazily scraping yourself up and down the door frame or discovers you have roped her best hairbrush to a wooden spoon and are frantically gouging it up and down your back with a weird look on your face like a cross between sheer panic and total heaven.

This is what it's like for animals who are not allowed to do the things they love or feel the need to do. It's the itch they can never scratch. All animals are born with some behaviours that are

what's called 'innate'. This means they are born needing to do something even if they don't know why. Other behaviours are learnt as they grow. For example, an innate behaviour for children appears to be constantly picking your nose, whereas a learnt one is getting a tissue and actually wiping it!

Innate behaviours help animals get a head start because they can do things without needing to be shown. One of the strongest and earliest innate behaviours you see is when animals suckle their mother's milk. Within minutes of being born, calves, lambs, kittens, puppies, rodents and human babies all start looking for their first warm drink of milk. They don't think about why and they don't need to but it gives them a great start because they get a full tummy and lots of goodness straight away.

The important thing to remember is that, even if we keep an animal in a way that means it doesn't need to do something any more, it will still feel

35

Chapter 6

THE NEED TO EXPRESS NORMAL BEHAVIOUR.

the urge to do it. It will still be the itch it can't scratch. A perfect example for animals such as gerbils and degus is digging.

You may well be about to give your digging-loving rodents a beautiful home to live in that they don't need to dig or make themselves. BUT millions of years of evolution have made these animals fanatical diggers. They LOVE it. Just because they don't need to dig a burrow they will still want to do it and feel frustrated and sad if they can't. It's our job as owners to find out all the things our pets naturally love to do and make it possible for them.

I will say quite a few times in this book that it is not OK to deprive an animal of one of its needs because it is difficult or inconvenient for us. I want you to think about how you like to live and the things you love to do. Can you imagine how you would feel if you had to live in your bedroom with

nothing else in it? In fact, give yourself a challenge. Find the smallest room in your house, a loo for instance so you can have a wee if you last long enough to need one! You're not allowed to take anything in there, no books, phones, iPads, tablets, pens, pencils, paper. Nothing at all. Time how long you can stay in there. I'd be amazed if any of you last an hour before you are terminally bored. If you are very determined you can let your mum or dad bring you food and drinks but they're not allowed to talk to you or stay for any length of time. Now imagine staying in there for two years, or for your human lifespan, 70 years! This is what it's like in a small, bare cage for our small furry pets. They'll survive but they certainly won't be happy.

We'll have a look at some of the things that all the small furries will enjoy and then we'll look at some of the things that might be a bit different.

Chewing

In pretty much every chapter we've mentioned that rodents have front teeth that grow throughout their whole lives. You'll hopefully have learnt that some of the food we give them is going to help keep their teeth healthy and short, but that won't be enough. In the wild they would be chewing through things to get to food, chewing up various things to make nests and bedding material, gnawing roots and bark on trees, and in some cases biting things including crunchy snail shells and tough insects. So you can guess that all your small furry pets need things to chew besides their food.

Something that's lovely for all of them are the branches of fruit trees, such as apples, pears and hazel. Make sure you know what tree they are from and that they haven't been sprayed with any chemicals or things like insecticides. The lovely wood will make a great natural chew. You can also be inventive and use branches like this to cover the top of the cage. For prey animals like this it makes them feel safe from birds of prey that might attack them from the sky and for climbers like rats and degus they can have some fun reaching the branches through the bars.

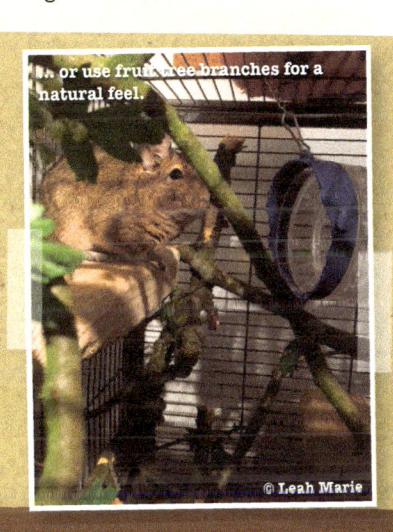

All rodents LOVE to chew.

You can use logs ...

... buy wooden toys from pet shops ...

... or use fruit tree branches for a natural feel.

Chapter 6

THE NEED TO EXPRESS NORMAL BEHAVIOUR.

The other thing that's great for all the rodents to chew is cardboard. Make sure it is untreated with chemicals and doesn't have any ink on it. I'm sure you will know that the easiest and most fun way to give small furries cardboard is by using loo rolls and kitchen rolls. As we've said, they all love hiding away in tunnels and logs and things so these tubes make great enrichment in more ways than one; hiding, exploring, hide-and-seek *and* chewing. For your bigger pets such as rats and degus you could use sturdy plastic pipes or a hollowed out wooden log.

Cardboard is everywhere these days and a great addition to any enclosure.

This is a good place to talk about bedding material. Once again, when you start trying to find out what's best there are lots of different opinions, which can be a bit confusing. I think the easiest thing is to stick to the things we know are really safe for all our pets and then it keeps life simple. We'll be saying extra about gerbils and their digging needs but all the small furries can have plain, shredded paper as bedding. You can also now buy lots of different types of paper-based bedding. It's safe if they chew it, soft enough to keep their little feet healthy and it can't get tangled around their legs or teeth. Dust-free, good quality hay is also great. Many rodents like to nibble the hay (and for animals such as degus it's an essential part of their diet) but it also makes a very natural bedding material as well. Lots of places sell recycled, shredded cardboard too and this can also make good, safe bedding for all these animals.

There are mixed thoughts on wood chips and shavings because they can cause breathing problems in some animals. It's best to avoid them to be on the safe side.

All rodents need a nest to hide away and rest in.

Nesting

All your small furries will want to make nests. It's where they would feel safe and secure to go to sleep. It's where they would have their babies and keep them safe while they grow. Remember, too, that we said small furries lose heat really quickly; well a nest is also the place they will really snuggle up to keep warm when it's cold outside. If you think about their fears and needs in the wild where predators are around you can start to imagine what sort of place is going to make a lovely nest. It needs to be dark and secluded, they need to have some lovely soft things to line it with to stay warm and it's best if it doesn't just have one small hole to get in and out. This is because if you have more than one pet they need to be able to avoid each other if one of them is feeling grumpy, and also because they are prey animals they will feel safer if there is more than one way out.

You can buy nest boxes from good pet shops and some cages will have them included. BUT, one of all kids' needs is to be creative and make things so this chapter is where you can really let loose and indulge your needs as well as your pets'. Clay flower pots make great nest places and if they have a large hole in the bottom and you put it on its side you instantly have two entrances. You can pick the size depending on the pet. You could put two almost facing each other with a little gap to get in so there is plenty of room to escape or snuggle. Coconut shells are also great nest places. Just make sure all the fruit is gone and they are clean and dry. Your mum or dad can help put extra holes in for escape routes.

Coconut shells make lovely natural hideaways.

39

Chapter 6

THE NEED TO EXPRESS NORMAL BEHAVIOUR.

Paper and hay make good nesting material but you can also give them a bit of luxury with plain tissue paper such as toilet roll, kitchen roll or normal tissues. You and your pets can have a lot of fun with this. Don't just put stuff in the nest for them, let them get busy and keep them active and stimulated. You can get an egg box, tube or the tissue box and stuff it full of tissues and hay. They can chew through it and wiggle inside or pull pieces out. They can then have all the fun of chewing up the pieces and putting them exactly where they want them. A little hayrack full of shredded kitchen roll also works well and the animals can pull pieces out as and when they want them without them getting wet or dirty.

Lots of animals such as rats will also enjoy sleeping in suspended beds, including hammocks. You can buy all sorts but you could also try making them too. It's a bit cheeky but you could always have a look online or wander around a pet shop to see what it has to offer and then have a family project to see if you can recreate some of the things.

Hammocks are very popular snuggle places.

It's very important NOT to give your small furries material such as cotton wool or thin cloth for them to make beds. These materials end up being pulled and chewed into long strands, which can cause serious problems in your pets' tummies and also in hamsters' cheek pouches.

Toys and exercise wheels

As well as tunnels there are lots of different toys you can get for your rodent pets. Climbers will love ropes and ladders and branches, and you can really let your imagination go wild. Try not to just put everything in all at once because, just like you and your toys, they can get boring. Try and rotate them every week or two so that the cage stays interesting. Lots of small furries love exercise wheels. It's very important that they are solid to avoid feet and tails getting trapped. You'll also need to make sure your wheel is definitely big enough for the pet you've chosen or they could hurt their backs.

Exercise balls used to be popular for pets like hamsters and mice but these days we know that animals can get exhausted by them because they can't escape or stop running easily. Balls are best avoided; just concentrate on having the biggest cage you can manage so that getting plenty of exercise isn't an issue. Remember that your rats and degus will need even more and must have exercise time out of their cage.

You can buy and make all sorts of fantastic toys for climbing and exploring.

Chapter 6

THE NEED TO EXPRESS NORMAL BEHAVIOUR.

Making food fun

Food bowls are very nice to have and convenient for us. Ideally you should always have two for the sociable pets. This means that if they're having a moody day they can always go to a bowl and not have to share it or squabble with the others. You might remember I said that things that are convenient for us are usually not the best idea for the pets. It's important to have a food bowl but you can also be inventive with feeding your pets and make life more interesting for them.

All animals in the wild spend hours and hours every day finding food. It's the balance of nature. Pets can easily get too fat if they are just given a heap of food in a bowl. We've already talked about feeding the right amounts and the right diet but you can make feeding time much more fun for them by hiding and scattering food. It's another great opportunity to be inventive. You can buy feeding toys that let food drop out of them as they get nudged but why not make something of your own? You could use an egg box like we said with the nesting materials but this time fill it with hay or tissue and add some pumpkin seeds or some of the pellets. For your omnivore pets you could hide dog food biscuits in a few different places around the cage and on all different levels.

Your pets will love foraging for food and exploring and working to find it just like they would in the wild. Don't hide things such as fresh veg or the egg/chicken/mealworms. If you forget where you put them it could get pretty revolting before too long!

Some rodents will enjoy 'fishing' in shallow water for healthy treats.

Sand/dust baths

Having a bath in sand or dust might not sound very appealing to creatures like us but it's a must for lots of animals such as elephants, chickens, gerbils and degus, to name only a few! Rolling around in sand and dust helps keep the skin, feathers and fur in top condition, gets rid of dead hair and skin and helps keep parasite numbers down in the wild. It also helps stop the coat getting too greasy and oily for pets.

Not all small furries need a sand bath but gerbils and degus really do. Don't just get dirt or dust out of your garden because it could make them ill, have bugs in it or be too wet. The easiest thing to do is buy sand from the pet shop. Often it's labelled for Chinchillas and this is ideal. Make sure they always have access to the bath so they can choose when to have one just like they would in the wild. You can use an open flat dish from home or buy one specially designed for it. If you're raiding the kitchen cupboards check with your mum or dad first; they might not appreciate a couple of degus in their best crockery!

Lots of animals have dust baths to keep their skin, fur and feathers healthy.

Dust baths aren't just important ... they're fun!

Gerbils (and other diggers!)

As we said in the last chapter, gerbils love to burrow and tuck themselves away so it's really important we give them the chance to do this. As we mentioned before, lots of good pet shops will sell enclosures with a deep, solid bottom so that your gerbils can make tunnels.

The best thing to give them is organic soil or peat. If you give them things such as shredded paper and Timothy hay as well they can use these to make the tunnels stronger. You can also give them cardboard tubes to hide in or put them in the peat for them to find and use. They can shred them if they want to and use the pieces, or use the whole tube. the peat for them to find and use. They can shred them if they want to and use the pieces, or use the whole tube.

Litter Training

You might be surprised to know that lots of small furries can be litter trained like a cat. Virtually all animals are very particular about where they go to the toilet and will especially always try to do it away from their food and bed. This is another reason why it's not fair to put them in little cages. Can you imagine eating your tea and going to bed in the school toilets? Yuk!

For bigger pets such as degus and rats, you can use dust-free cat litter in a small litter tray. If they go to the toilet somewhere else just put a little bit of the soiled bedding in the litter tray and they will start to use that area. For hamsters and mice, you can try picking something easily cleanable such as a small jar on its side and put some of the soiled bedding in there with some shredded paper or cardboard. This should encourage them to start to go in the same place. Make sure your toilet area is well away from their food and bed or it simply won't work, for obvious reasons. Rodents might not use the toilet or litter tray all the time because they will still do things such as territory marking but you can usually get them almost fully trained and make cleaning up a bit easier.

Chapter 6

THE NEED TO EXPRESS NORMAL BEHAVIOUR.

© Pets at Home

You can start with a great cage ...

So there you have it, how to make your pets' lives and homes as enriched as possible. Letting animals behave in as natural a way as possible is so, so important. I know I've said it before but I really want you to enjoy doing this. Children are masters of imagination and creativity so let your imagination go wild and you and your pets will have a LOT of fun in the process.

In general the happier you are the healthier you are and this is true for our pets too. However, of course, sometimes we all get poorly for one reason or another. So now we know all the ways to make our animals happy we had better see what can still go wrong and how you can help to keep them as *healthy* as possible too.

© Becky Levy

© Emily Skipp

© Jade Hirons

... and make it SUPER!

Chapter 7

THE NEED TO BE PROTECTED FROM PAIN, INJURY AND DISEASE.

We're counting on you!

Every person and every animal gets poorly or hurt from time to time. That's just a simple fact of being alive. I always tell my daughters that their bumped shins and skinned knees are a good sign they've been having plenty of fun. We have already talked about what amazing machines bodies are and one of their most amazing abilities is how they can heal and recover from injuries and disease. But you'll all know already that there are lots of illnesses and injuries that bodies can't cope with and that they need extra help with. It's not just about getting help for your pets when they are poorly or hurt, it's very important to find out all the ways you can stop them getting ill in the first place.

One of the most important things when it comes to keeping pets healthy is observation and knowing what's normal. Children are way more observant than adults, so you can put yourself in charge of keeping a close eye on your pets. At some point all your animals will need to be handled for things such as being moved when you clean the cage, if they come out for exercise time and when they go to the vet. If you get them used to it from an early age you'll have more fun with them, they'll be much less likely to bite you and less likely to struggle to get away and hurt themselves in the process.

You might be surprised to know that lots of animals, even big ones such as dogs and cats, hate being mauled, hugged and carried about. They find it very frightening and lots of animals don't show affection like humans do so they find us a bit weird and scary when we want to cuddle them all the time. Small furries are prey animals and they are tiny compared to you, so at first you can imagine that you will seem like the scariest giant imaginable. Some of their main predators in the wild are birds of prey that swoop from the sky so if they are picked up from above they feel like they've been caught and will be more likely to try to get away.

Chapter 7

THE NEED TO BE PROTECTED FROM PAIN, INJURY AND DISEASE.

It's a good idea to go to your vet as soon as possible when you get your small furries. Your vet can make sure there is nothing wrong with them but most importantly you can ask him or her to show you how to pick them up and hold them safely. You should also take your pets to the vet twice a year for a check-up even if they seem OK. If you spot things early you can do more to help them and your vet will notice things that you might not and can also check if your pets are the right weight. It might seem silly to take them every six months but for an animal that only lives two or three years like a hamster it would be like you only going for a check up every 30 years!

All small furries need handling slightly differently so do ask your vet how to do it. In general though you must NEVER catch your pets by the tail. To start with just spend lots of time near the cage so your pets get used to the sight, sound and *smell* of you. Offer tasty, healthy treats without trying to pick them up so they get used to your hand and your fingers. Then you can start to put food on your palm so they climb on and get used to being lifted. Always approach from the side, always stay quiet and calm and don't make sudden movements. If you are ever in any doubt, ask a grown-up to help you.

Small furries, with the right diet and environment, tend to be pretty healthy, robust little creatures. For example, they don't need vaccinations like people and many animals do against serious infectious diseases. But you may have guessed from some of the things we've learned so far that there are still certain things they need or problems they could be prone to when kept as pets. We'll start with things that are possible problems for all of them and then look at how they might be different.

Teeth!!

Seeing as it's the teeth that actually make rodents rodents we'd better mention them again here. I'm sure those fabulous brains of yours will have realised from the last few chapters that if we don't get the diet right and we don't give our pets plenty of good stuff to chew then their teeth can be a disaster.

> **RODENT FACT:**
> Most adult rodents have teeth that are yellow to orange in colour, not shiny white like our teeth. This is completely normal for them. In fact, for some small furries, white teeth can be a sign of health problems such as low vitamin levels.

Yellow teeth are normal for most rodents.

You might notice overgrown teeth poking out of your pet's lip but sometimes the teeth curl inwards and can cause very serious damage inside the mouth and lots of pain. This is easy to miss and it's a good reason for regular vet visits.

Always check to see that your pet is actually eating and not just at the food bowl. They might be wanting to eat but can't because of teeth problems. Make sure you see them actually take something into their mouth every day. They can lose weight really quickly if they stop eating and die within a few days. If you're good at noticing things you'll hopefully see if they are starting to look thin. We mentioned the opposite problem in Chapter 3, obesity, and it's time to mention that again. Learning about something called body condition score (BCS) is a good way to judge if something is too fat, too thin or just right.

Some overgrown teeth are quite obvious ...

... but if they overgrow inside the mouth they are easily missed.

47

Chapter 7

THE NEED TO BE PROTECTED FROM PAIN, INJURY AND DISEASE.

Obesity and body condition score

Vets and lots of people who work with animals use body condition score (BCS) to talk about whether an animal is the right weight. We use a scale of 1 to 5, where 1 is terribly thin, 2 is a bit on the thin side, 3 is perfect, 4 is a bit fat and 5 is very fat or obese. In the last few years sadly humans and animals have all got fatter in general. Nowadays in many places, when you ask someone to judge whether a normal animal is fat or not, lots of people think they are too thin. We've got so used to seeing fat animals that we think it's normal. It's not. And it's something we really need to change. An animal with a BCS of 3, which is perfect, will have a visible waist and you should be able to feel the shoulder blades, ribs, spine and hips without any problems and with just a thin covering on them. Whenever your animal goes to the vet, always ask them what they think about its body condition so that you can judge it correctly.

Being too fat is not pleasant for animals. We don't want our animals to be hungry but overfeeding them is just as cruel as starving an animal. Being too fat definitely shortens life, causes diseases in some animals such as diabetes, puts extra strain on the heart, muscles and joints, and causes high blood pressure.

... compared to some beautifully slim wild ones.

Some unhealthily fat pet rodents ...

Do you remember way back in Chapters 2 and 3 we said that rodents are coprophagic? This means they eat their soft poo straight from their bottom and have another go at digesting all the nutrients. For animals like this being too fat is especially bad. If they can't reach their bottom because they are too fat they can't eat the soft poo and they can quickly get covered in poo. This is not pleasant at all and they won't be able to clean themselves either because they can't reach. Please don't overfeed your animals and make sure they have lots of opportunities to run, climb, explore and exercise.

Bumblefoot

This might sound like a character from Harry Potter but it's actually a horrible, painful disease that small furries can easily get if their cage or enclosure is not right. The fancy, sciency name for it is pododermatitis, but we'll stick to bumblefoot because it's easier to say!

Bumblefoot is what happens when small furries are kept on hard floors or wire-bottomed cages. They have sensitive little feet and in the wild live on soft, grassy plains and sandy soils. When they have wire to walk on or not enough bedding their feet get little cuts and grazes. These get infected and the bacteria that invade the cuts make painful abscesses and sore feet. These will make your small furries limp, be very miserable and they can be very difficult to treat. As always, prevention is better than cure. Being the brilliant detectives you are, I'm sure your small furries will have rodent palaces to live in and beautifully looked after feet but now you know another reason why fact-finding is so important.

Bumblefoot is very painful and very hard to treat.

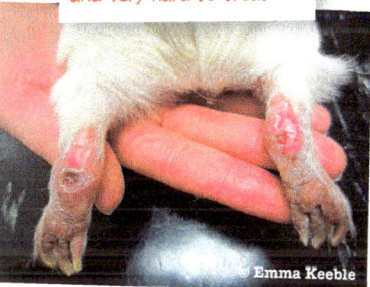

Respiratory disease

This is another long phrase but it means breathing problems and infections in the lungs. Lots of rodents easily get respiratory diseases especially if their environment is not right. Rats are most likely to get problems but all rodents can be affected. If you use dusty bedding the dust clogs up the lungs when they breathe it in and makes them very ill. If they are in a draughty place or somewhere that the temperature changes a lot in the course of a day they can also get ill, a bit like you catching a cold. If you don't clean their cage out often enough the chemicals in urine can build up and make them very poorly. The smell of urine is usually caused by something called ammonia. This chemical smells really horrible and can cause lots of problems if it builds up. Humans often don't notice how smelly a cage is because we are quite high up and our noses are not very sensitive. Try putting your nose at rodent level and have a good sniff!

You might not be able to stop every respiratory problem in your pets because they could catch a bug just like we do but most of their problems are caused by a dirty or badly located cage. This is something you can definitely prevent happening. Having a good environment isn't just all about having fun and behaving naturally, it's really important for preventing diseases as well.

Chapter 7

THE NEED TO BE PROTECTED FROM PAIN, INJURY AND DISEASE.

Tail injuries

We've already said that you must never catch or pick your pet rodents up by their tails. Degus and gerbils especially can lose some or all of the skin from their tails if this happens. Sometimes the damage is so bad they have to have their tail amputated (cut off). Rodents with tails use them to balance when they climb and rats and mice use them to help control how hot they are, so losing their tail is a big problem. You should also know that for some reason people have bred some rats so that they don't have tails. This is very unnatural and means they can't balance and they can't control their body temperature very well. Do not buy tailless rats.

Tail injuries don't heal well and sometimes pets lose their tails completely.

For all rodents it's also really important to make sure things such as their exercise wheels are solid so their tails can't get trapped and injured. Damaged tails can get infected and sometimes die or fall off, or need to be amputated. Dirty bedding and cages can also cause sores and infections in the tail, so keep the cages nice and clean. We'll be looking at that routine and what you need to do in the next chapter.

Diabetes in degus

We mentioned when we looked at food that degus are very prone to a disease called diabetes. This disease is related to sugar in the diet and degus can't tolerate sugar at all, even the natural sugars in fruits. Diabetes can kill animals so it's really important to prevent it. For animals such as cats and humans as well as degus, staying slim really helps prevent diabetes. For degus as well though, it's really important that their diet has as little sugar as possible in it. If you need help remembering, just go back to Chapter 3 and remind yourself. Lots of hay, grass and leaves is most important for them and all their dry food and treats need to be sugar-free.

For degus just remember grass, hay, grass, hay, more grass and more hay!

Wet-tail in hamsters

This is a very serious disease that is common in hamsters. It's most common in very young animals or when they move home or something happens that stresses them. Stress in animals isn't really like us saying we're stressed about our homework or an exam, but it has the same effects inside. All sorts of stress can make animals and humans poorly because it can stop their immune system working properly. Your immune system is like a little army inside your body that fights off germs. For animals, stress is caused by things such as leaving their family to go to a new home, a change in diet, a dirty cage or being too overcrowded with not enough space for all the animals.

In hamsters, stress often leads to wet-tail. This is diarrhoea caused by a certain bacteria and one of the first and most common signs is a wet tail area, hence the name. Wet-tail can easily kill a hamster in a couple of days but the sooner you spot it the better, so being observant is really important. If you notice signs of this you must get your hamster straight to a vet because it's a real emergency.

Keeping the cage clean and avoiding the things that might stress your animal that we mentioned will help prevent it in the first place. Sometimes you won't be able to prevent it and early treatment is by far the best option.

Cheek pouch problems in hamsters

Pouches are very useful but can cause problems.

Cheek pouches sometimes cause problems. The two main problems are impacted pouches and everted pouches. Impacted means crammed full of stuff. It's very useful having cheek pouches like shopping bags but sometimes it can be very difficult to unpack your shopping! Some foods and bedding materials can get wedged in the pouches and the hamsters can't get them emptied. This means that food and other material can start to rot and damage the pouches, and this can be quite serious. We said before that bedding such as cotton wool and cloths should be avoided and these can cause serious pouch impactions as well as gut problems.

Occasionally, even with the right food you can get impacted pouches and some hamsters seem more likely to get them than others but no one really knows why. If you notice that one or both sides of your hamster's face are always swollen, or your hamster is constantly trying to empty the pouches but nothing is coming out, take it to your vet. Usually your vet will be able to massage the contents out but if not he or she can decide what is best to do next.

The pink fleshy thing you can see under this hamster's mouth is an everted pouch.

Everted means turned inside out. Sometimes hamsters' pouches turn inside out as they are emptied. They need to have an anaesthetic at the vets to get them to go back in. If you ever see a pink sac hanging out of your hamster's mouth, this is an everted pouch. Get the animal to the vet straight away before it gets damaged.

Chapter 7

THE NEED TO BE PROTECTED FROM PAIN, INJURY AND DISEASE.

Are your small furries healthy?

The things we've mentioned so far are the big things to be aware of when it comes to having pet small furries but there are all sorts of diseases, conditions and injuries that can happen. If you want to learn about every single one then you should do your homework, work hard and become a vet because I haven't got room for all of it here! As we've said lots of times, the best way to keep your pets healthy in general is to be observant and know what's normal so you can quickly spot when things are wrong.

RODENT FACT:

Lots of prey animals such as small furries don't show pain and illness in the same way as predators. If they limp or whine, or cry in the wild, they will just attract attention and make it obvious they might be weak enough to be caught and eaten. This means lots of prey animals are very good at hiding when they are poorly or hurt and being brave. Sometimes they just go quiet or stop moving around much. It takes a good detective to notice when they are off colour or hurt. Knowing what's normal is the key.

Things to watch for in your small furries themselves

- **Bright eyes** Watch out for runny eyes or discharge, swelling round the eyelids or redness. These could be signs of infections or scratches but it can also be because of tooth root problems.

- **Clean, healthy nose** No snot or mucus coming from either side, no sores.

- **Shiny, clean fur** All animals, including humans, can get parasites such as fleas, lice and mites. If you see scratching, bald patches, dandruff or scabs they could have a problem and need to go to the vet straight away. Look out for wet fur under the chin. This could be a sign of drooling and dribbling, and tooth problems. Just as we said with the tails, some people have made breeds of small furries that are hairless. Once again, this is totally unnatural and will make them much more likely to get scratched and injured, and get infections. It will also make it much harder for them to stay warm. Do NOT buy hairless rodents!

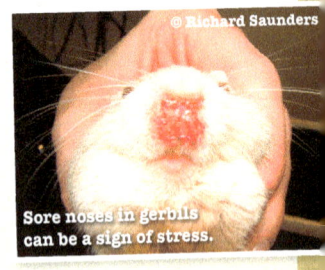

© Richard Saunders

Sore noses in gerbils can be a sign of stress.

Smaller animals such as small furries can get weak and ill very quickly, so if you are ever worried then take them to the vet. Your vet won't think you're silly if there's nothing wrong. It's always better to be safe than sorry.

Dandruff, scabs or bald patches could be a sign of parasites such as mites.

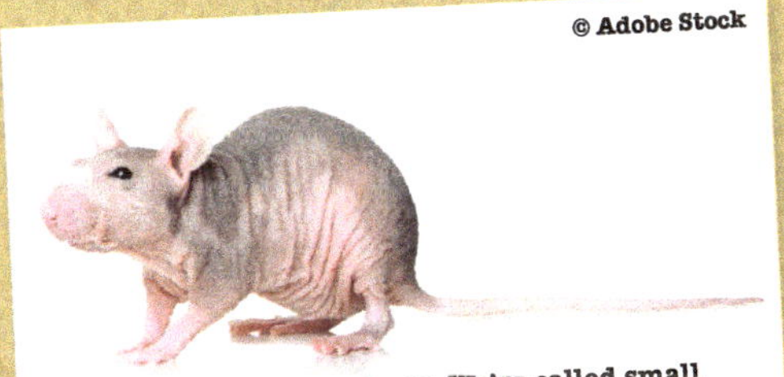

© Emma Keeble

© Adobe Stock

Do NOT buy hairless rodents. We're called small FURRIES for a reason!

RODENT FACT:

Some bald patches are totally normal. Syrian hamsters have a dark-skinned, bald patch on each of their sides near their back legs. Gerbils (and dwarf hamsters) have one on their tummies. These are totally normal glands and help with things such as territory marking and finding a mate. If you're ever unsure, take them to your vet. We're used to seeing normal things and can put your mind at rest. Better to be safe than sorry …

Comfortable, clean ears If your small furries' ears seem dirty or itchy, or you see them keep shaking their heads, they could have ear mites or an ear infection. This sometimes also gives them a head tilt. Time for a trip to the vet.

Body Condition Score Try and keep it a perfect 3.

Make sure your small furries don't have any sore patches anywhere You need to check all over and on their joints and feet.

Make sure their nails are not overgrown Depending on how much exercise your small furries do and the places they live, they will occasionally need their nails cut. Your vet or vet nurse will be happy to tell you if they need doing.

Check for poo around the bottom every day and twice in the summer Flies are attracted to poo and dirty bedding and can lay maggot eggs on your pets or in their cages, which is definitely best avoided.

Normal breathing As we have said, small furries don't like extremes of temperature, draughts and damp or dirty cages. They can easily get chest infections, so try to get used to what normal breathing is like. If they are breathing very fast, making a noise when they breathe or seem to be putting a lot of effort into it they should go to a vet.

Lumps and bumps All rodents, but especially rats, are prone to tumours. Many animals (and humans) can get tumours. These are growths and can appear anywhere on or inside the body. Some of them are nothing to worry about but some are serious cancers, so always get lumps on your pets (and yourself!) checked out. Mammary tumours are common so keep an eye on their tummies too.

© Emma Keeble

Rats are quite prone to tumours like this.

Look out for odd behaviour This could be anything from being 'a bit quiet' to hunched, not eating, not moving around as normal, stiff, floppy, teeth grinding, or sneezing; basically, anything out of the ordinary. If you see any weird or unusual behaviour, get your small furries to the vet as soon as you can.

Chapter 7

THE NEED TO BE PROTECTED FROM PAIN, INJURY AND DISEASE.

Things to watch for in your small furries' surroundings

- **Normal faeces (poo) and urine (wee)** If you see the soft sticky faeces a lot of the time then it could be a sign of trouble. Diarrhoea is a definite sign that all is not well. Once again, you'll soon get used to what's normal for your small furries. If you don't look, you don't know! All rodents, but especially gerbils, can get a disease called Tyzzer's disease. This is very serious and causes liver problems, but diarrhoea is one of the first signs so keep an eye out. Any diarrhoea is a big problem for small furries because they get dehydrated so quickly. Straight to the vet if you see it.

- **Dropped or half-chewed food** If you find clumps of half-chewed food it could be a sign that one or more of your small furries has tooth problems.

Don't panic about all these things; the more you get to know your small furries, the sooner and more easily you'll spot the odd things. The better an owner you are, the healthier your small furries will be and hopefully the fewer trips to the vet you'll need. Remember that you can't get small furries and just forget about them. You need to be around them at least once a day, check them over and make sure they are safe, protected and well. If in doubt, ask your vet.

Now you have all the facts about wild small furries and you know how to keep them happy as well as healthy. So it must be time for even more fact-finding, some virtual reality and some good old maths. Basically, it's time to actually answer that crucial question:

Are small furry rodents the right pets for me and my family?

Chapter 8

ARE SMALL FURRY RODENTS THE RIGHT PET FOR ME AND MY FAMILY?

In this chapter we're going to crunch some numbers and you're going to have to start investigating facts from some other places besides this book. We're also going to embark on a virtual month of being a rodent owner. You might feel silly but it's a brilliant way of checking if you actually do have what it takes to be a dedicated owner of small furries. You can do it all by yourself or you can involve the whole family in the decisions, care and sums.

If you find yourself, towards the end of the virtual month, getting a bit bored with pretending to check over, feed, handle and clean out a teddy once or twice a day remember this; depending on which small furry you have they could live for up to ten years, but even mice live for more than a year so you need to get used to it!

Did someone say maths?!

Week One — How Much??!

We'll spend the first week finding out some costs to ease you into it gently. Things such as buying the cage might seem like a one-off but bear in mind that over the course of two to ten years some things might wear out and need replacing, so a bit of reserve cash is always needed. Things such as toys are good to rotate or renew, so try to get an idea of the cost of, say, three average toys and allow that amount every month.

Now is also the time to consider right from the outset how much room you have. If you don't have the space for the big cage or you've decided the house is not the right place for small furries then you might not need to go much further and can avoid the painful maths! So, assuming you have the room, here's a place to start filling in those numbers. The boxes coloured in green are either one-off costs or those that will only need to be repeated rarely. This will help you and your family get an idea of how much your initial outlay is likely to be compared to ongoing costs. Don't forget though that virtually everything will need to be paid for at the start, so add everything together for your start-up costs!

55

Chapter 8

ARE SMALL FURRY RODENTS THE RIGHT PET FOR ME AND MY FAMILY?

Things to find out from the pet shop/adoption centre or the internet

Item	Cost £
The small furries! Please don't forget to check local adoption centres. There are always plenty of animals looking for a new home. Remember to multiply the cost for the number of small furries you are planning to have.	
Cage or gerbilarium. Remember to look back at our minimum sizes depending on the pets you're thinking of and make sure you have enough room for more than one animal for the social species.	
Exercise area materials. You'll need to think about this for rats and degus. Talk to your family about the best thing to build it out of or whether you'll let them have a whole room.	
Bedding. Try to find out roughly how long a bag will last so you can work out monthly costs for your family.	
Good quality hay – essential for degus but great nesting material and food for many others. Try to find out roughly how long a bag will last so you can work out monthly costs for your family.	
Pellets or mix. Try to find out roughly how long a bag will last so you can work out monthly costs for family.	
Veg and occasional dog biscuits/mealworms for those that need it. You'll need to ask your parents this one. They'll need to buy extra veg to make sure your small furries get a good variety.	
Food bowls or scatter balls. It's wise to have more than one little bowl so you can avoid fighting.	
Water bottles.	
Hay racks and racks for nesting material if you're going to provide one.	
Toys and chews. Find out how often chews will need replacing and get an idea how much toys cost to allow for occasional replacements. Some of the big enrichment toys such as hammocks, ladders, ropes and nest boxes might last a long time but budget to keep it fresh and interesting.	
Total	

Things to find out from your vet

Procedure	Cost £
Normal consultation and routine check-ups. Many people think small furries are cheaper to have examined by a vet when they are poorly but some vets will charge the same as for a dog or cat so it's worth finding out what that cost is. Make sure you ask what the average cost of treatments are for common things such as a course of antibiotics.	
Nail trim. Find out how often a vet feels it usually needs doing. Some small furries may never need this done but it's worth finding out.	
Total from this and the last page added together	

These numbers may be a bit mind-bogglingly big when you look at them but that's why I wanted you to do it. There is no such thing as a cheap pet. Obviously you will have worked out that once you're all set up your monthly costs may be much more manageable but don't forget about vets' fees and unexpected problems. Small furries are definitely cheaper than some pets but they will still cost between £700 and £3,000, or possibly more, over their lifetime depending on which one you have. And for the social ones you'll need more than one.

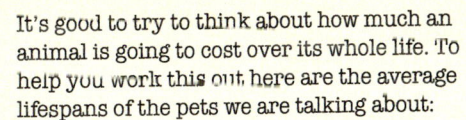

A little help

It's good to try to think about how much an animal is going to cost over its whole life. To help you work this out, here are the average lifespans of the pets we are talking about:

Degus:	6-10 years
Gerbils:	2-5 years
Rats and hamsters:	2-3 years
Mice:	1-2 years

Chapter 8

ARE SMALL FURRY RODENTS THE RIGHT PET FOR ME AND MY FAMILY?

Week Two – Handle with Care

This week you are going to spend time and energy devoted to your new (pretend!) small furries and getting to know them. It's important to get your small furries used to being handled right from a young age. As we said in the last chapter, this will help them feel safe and secure with you and not feel threatened. If they are happy being handled gently they will be much less likely to scratch or bite you and also less likely to hurt themselves thrashing to get away from you. It will also make them feel less stressed when they need to go to the vet and be handled by strangers.

This week you will need to spend about half an hour each morning and evening getting to know your small furries. Practice how you would approach and pick them up. Remember to stay quiet and move gently and calmly. Look online and see if you can find videos of how to handle your chosen small furries. You should be able to catch them, hold them safely and learn how to gently examine them to make sure they are well.

Most of the time should be used to just hold them gently or let them walk over your hands to help with bonding, and to start with you might find it best just to spend some time quietly near your small furries so they get used to your smell and the look of you. Offering a tasty, healthy treat out of their ration when you handle them will help your small furries see you as a real goodie rather than a possible predator! Try to look out for signs of when your small furries have had enough. All animals vary and your small furries might not be interested in cuddles from you. If they are like this remember to respect their needs and be happy just to watch them having fun together.

As well as the contact time, once or twice a day depending on the time of year you will also need to examine them for all the things we said to look out for in Chapter 7. You will need to briefly look at their bottoms and their underneath for poo or sores but try not to take too long to do this because small furries don't feel safe on their backs. When you've got your real small furries, if you decide to go ahead, this will be the time when you'll really start to get to know how they feel and how they behave. If you've got degus or rats, once they are used to you and being handled you can start to let them have their exercise time. You need to be sure you can safely get them back to their cage without frightening them or chasing them. By handling them every day you'll soon spot when things are not right and if they feel skinnier or fatter than they should.

Here is a table to fill in for this week. Once you are in the swing of things you'll find that most of the body check becomes part of your normal handling time and you add the bottom check as an extra. Oh yes, and don't forget to wash your hands afterwards!

Job/Day	Monday	Tuesday	Wednesday	Thursday	Friday	Saturday	Sunday
Time nearby, handling AM							
Time nearby, handling PM							
Full body check AM or PM							
Bottom check (should be done twice daily in summer)							
Front teeth and claw check (once a week)	x	x	x	x	x	x	

Week Three — Fed, Watered and Neat as a Pin!

This week you'll be doing the dirty work! As well as feeding and checking the water is fresh and clean you'll be learning about cleaning up. It's a rare person who *really* enjoys cleaning anything so you can be forgiven for not looking forward to this but it is a huge part of pet keeping. There is no getting away from the fact that some of what goes in has to come out and it is up to you to clear it up! Handling poo and sometimes wee can make you poorly so you need to make sure you know all about hygiene. Always wear gloves to clean your cage (and exercise area if necessary) and always wash your hands afterwards. Look back at Chapter 3 if you need to remind yourself about how much of which foods to give if you can't remember.

Of course, you still don't have any small furries so this week is about setting aside the time you need as if you had to do these jobs. Why not get your mum or dad to give you a boring job to do that would take about the same amount of time? Clean the bathroom, including the loo, empty all the bins or do the ironing. You'll get an idea of the more boring and yucky side of being a pet owner and you'll get massive brownie points at the same time.

Checklist for this week;

Job/Day	Monday	Tuesday	Wednesday	Thursday	Friday	Saturday	Sunday
Check/give food AM							
Check/give food PM							
Give fresh water and clean bottle AM							
Check/freshen water and clean bottle if necessary PM							
Remove uneaten fresh food once daily							
Remove soiled bedding once daily and top up bedding and nest material if needed							
Wash food bowls once daily (more often if dirty)							
Clean out whole cage and replace bedding once weekly. (For gerbils this needs to be done about every 3 weeks)	x	x	x	x	x	x	
Check toys, chews and enrichment and replace if necessary (once a week)	x	x	x	x	x	x	

Chapter 8

ARE SMALL FURRY RODENTS THE RIGHT PET FOR ME AND MY FAMILY?

> This is also the time to look online and find out about which plants, veg and fruits are safe and which are poisonous for the pet you're thinking about. Here is a place to make your lists.

Safe	Poisonous

Week Four — EVERYTHING!!

And now for the grand finale. This week you will need to find an hour most days and more at the weekends in your hectic schedule to devote to your new pets. Fill in the rather large table below and add in your ongoing costs at the bottom. Most of all, try to enjoy it because if you do get some small furries you're going to be doing this for years, not weeks, and possibly, if you have degus, even until you leave home!

Job/Day	Monday	Tuesday	Wednesday	Thursday	Friday	Saturday	Sunday
Time nearby, handling AM							
Time nearby, handling PM							
Full body check AM or PM							
Bottom check (should be done twice daily in summer)							
Front teeth and claw check (once a week)	x	x	x	x	x	x	
Check/give food AM							
Check/give food PM							
Give fresh water and clean bottle AM							
Check/freshen water and clean bottle if necessary PM							
Remove uneaten fresh food once daily							
Remove soiled bedding once daily and top up bedding and nest material if needed							
Wash food bowls once daily (more often if dirty)							
Clean out whole cage and replace bedding once weekly. (For gerbils this needs to be done about every 3 weeks)	x	x	x	x	x	x	
Check toys, chews and enrichment and replace if necessary (once a week)	x	x	x	x	x	x	

Chapter 8

ARE SMALL FURRY RODENTS THE RIGHT PET FOR ME AND MY FAMILY?

Time for the Family Debate

Over the last few weeks, and having read the rest of the book, you should now have some idea of what keeping small furries is actually about. If you're like most people you'll probably be quite shocked. It's very rare for people to realise just how much time and money is needed to look after pets well. Anyone can look after pets badly but I hope that now you will most definitely not be one of them!

You've probably been talking to your family about things as you've gone along but if not now is the time to do that. You can call a meeting and present your facts, like all the best detectives do, because now you really do have everything you need to answer that question. And to answer it honestly.

Things you might want to talk about at your family meeting

- If you are under 16, someone else in your family will be legally obliged to provide all these things for your small furries and they need to agree to that!

- Do small furries, from what you've learned, tick the boxes of what you'd like in a pet? If you thought they were something different don't be ashamed to change your mind. That's the whole point of finding out all about them – to make the right choices.

- Can your family afford the costs you've found out? Lots of people get embarrassed talking about money but now is not the time to be shy. If you can't afford it, don't get any.

- Did you have the time, energy and room to provide for all the things your imaginary pets needed? And if so, could you do that for two to ten years? Depending on your age and your pet choice you may well be moving on before your small furries die so your family will need to carry on where you leave off. Are they willing to that?

- Is the whole family on board with the idea?

Well, what's the answer?

© Adobe Stock

I hope that after all your hard work you finally get the answer you wanted, but what about if you didn't? Time to ask the next question: **What if the answer is no?**

Chapter 9

WHAT IF THE ANSWER IS NO?

As we said all the way back in Chapter 1, you should never ask yourself what sort of pet you want, you should ask yourself what sort of pet you can care for properly. The fact-finding you've done up to now will hopefully have helped you work out if small furries are animals you can keep healthy and, just as importantly, happy. As I said at the end of the last chapter, there is absolutely no shame in finding out the answer is no. That is the point of your mission and the book, to help you and your family make the right and responsible choice. Not only will you have happy pets but hopefully you'll have pets that make *you* happy too. Very often, pets get given away because they were bought on an impulse with no research. In the case of small furries, it can easily happen too. If kept alone (the social ones) and never handled they can be very unfriendly and unhappy animals. They will not be very nice pets through no fault of their own, simply because they are misunderstood and poorly cared for. This becomes a vicious circle, the children don't want to touch them and they get neglected or given away.

Did you say NO?!

So if you have done your numbers and learnt your facts, and decided that small furries are not the right pet for you or your family, then that is just as worthwhile as deciding to go ahead and buy some. A massive WELL DONE either way. You should be very proud of yourself. If you found that small furries didn't tick your boxes or you couldn't tick theirs it doesn't necessarily mean you can't have a pet; we just need to look at some alternatives depending on what you were struggling with.

There's a brilliant animal charity called the PDSA and they've come up with a great way to think about having pets – and that is to think PETS! That is Place, Exercise, Time and Spend. Going through those four things for whichever animal you are thinking about is a good way to decide if you can keep them properly. On their website they have a great tool to help people find the right pet for their own situation, so do have a look at that as well. For now we'll go one step at a time through PETS and see what other pets might suit you best! Remember that this is just a pointer. You will still need to thoroughly research any pet you are considering. Just because one animal may need less room or be cheaper to keep, there may be other things about it that might put you or your family off.

Chapter 9

WHAT IF THE ANSWER IS NO?

Place

Small furries need more room than many people expect, especially degus and rats. We are still too used to picturing the tiny cages that so many pet shops and online shops sell. You may have been very surprised to see just how much they need, especially if you fancy keeping a few of them. So here are some pet ideas that might be better.

Rabbits and guinea pigs.

These need way more space than the small furries but they can be kept outside in some climates. You might find that if you have a good-sized garden but your mum wasn't keen on a big cage in the house that these might suit you better. You should know, though, that rabbits and guinea pigs also have lots of other needs and do need a lot of care and attention, so you must do your research before rushing to the pet shop or adoption centre.

Different small furries.

It might sound obvious but if you were planning on rats or degus and you didn't realise how much room and exercise they need, you could just go for a smaller option such as mice, hamsters or gerbils.

Cats and dogs.

These may be very different to what you were originally considering and in some ways need lots more space than small furries, but they are still worth thinking about. Maybe your house didn't have space for a large enough cage. As cats and dogs live in the house and just go outside for fun and exercise they might actually be better for you. Both cats and dogs have very complex needs, so make sure you can provide for those too.

Fish.

Fish are very calming, beautiful animals to watch and are very popular with lots of people. A fish tank could be much smaller than a degu cage but if you look into fish always consider how much room they would like because a tiny bowl can be just as bad as a little cage. Please, if you do look into keeping fish, find out about where they come from. Some will be taken from the wild and this could be very damaging to the place they come from.

Exercise

In the case of small furries, exercise is kind of included in space because you need to give them the space and enrichment to exercise when they want. I like to think of this 'E' as energy as well. It takes a lot of energy to care for pets properly. That energy could well be walking a dog or playing with a cat but it could also be the energy you need to keep your small furries' run new and interesting. It could be the energy you need to drag yourself into a cold garden to handle and groom your rabbits every day. If when you did your virtual month that all seemed like a lot of hassle what else could you consider?

All pets need some commitment from you but some need less interaction or different interaction that might be easier. Rabbits and guinea pigs will need all the same handling and care as small furries and more when it comes to energy expenditure, so are probably best avoided. Dogs in general needs lots of energy devoted to them and their exercise, so if you're a bit on the lazy side steer clear of them too!

Different small furries.

As we said before, you might be able to just change your idea of which pet you were considering. Some small furries such as hamsters and mice are happy not to be fussed over and might quite like being left alone. All pets need to be used to being handled but not all of them really need it and might prefer not to have it if given the choice. You'll still need to expend some energy looking after them but we'll look at that next.

Cats.

Cats are like teenagers; they're difficult to understand, they don't communicate well, they spend a lot of time sleeping and are likely to lash out at you for no apparent reason! Depending on the type of cat you have, you'll often find that they like to interact strictly on their own terms and will come to you when they feel like having some affection. In this way they might need less from you than small furries.

Fish.

Fish might be a good alternative but make sure you know what sort of fish you are taking on and how much you will need to do to keep the environment right for them.

Chapter 9

WHAT IF THE ANSWER IS NO?

Time

In your virtual month, especially in the last week, you should have found that your small furries need a good one to two hours of your time *every* day and sometimes more. This might not sound a lot to many people but when you actually have to do it day in and day out it can quickly become difficult to find the time. You probably won't be surprised to hear that lots of non-pet detective owners don't realise the time needed until it's too late and pretty soon we're back to that neglected and forgotten pet.

Time is very precious to lots of people. We live in busy times. Lots of parents work, lots of kids do a million after-school activities and weekends disappear in the blink of an eye. Trying to find even a spare hour every day can be a massive headache for any family, even if you share the work. All pets need some time commitment from you and it's definitely worth considering right now if you found time an issue at all in your virtual month. It's better not to have a pet than to have an unhappy, badly looked after one.

Time and energy go hand in hand. If you struggled to find the time for small furries then dogs, guinea pigs and rabbits will be the same. As we said with cats and some of the small furries, in some ways they may need less time. It will vary depending on the animal and, as always, research will be important. For example, if you have a long-haired cat you might need hours to try to keep its coat under control but if you end up with an independent, short-haired moggie some of them pretty much look after themselves. All the small furries will need some time for cleaning and feeding, and again that will vary depending on the animal and the size of their cage, how they live and how dirty they are! Fish could well be another good alternative but, as with the energy required, some such as marine fish might need more time than others to keep their tank exactly right.

Time is a precious commodity, and so is money ...

Spend

The cost of keeping pets is probably the most massively underestimated thing of all when it comes to owners. Stuff including bedding, toys, and cages are easy things to work out and think about but people always forget about vets' bills and quite shockingly, the cost of food. Feeding an animal for two to ten years can make a big hole in your wallet!

The PDSA do a report every year called the PAW report that looks at how well animals are cared for. They ask lots and lots of owners how much they thought it would cost to look after a dog, cat or rabbit for the whole of its life. Most people thought it would cost £1,000—£5,000 for a dog when in fact, depending on the breed it can be up to a staggering £31,000! Most people gave the same answer of £1,000—£5,000 for a cat but the average is actually often a whopping £17,000. The average rabbit costs £9,000 but when owners were asked what they thought it would be nearly all of them said about £1,000. As we said, small furries will cost roughly between £700 and £3,000.

You can see why people are shocked when they actually get the animals. Money is another big reason that pets get given away. As I said, some people are shy when it comes to talking about money but if you're thinking of getting a pet it's absolutely vital you find out how much it is likely to cost and make sure your family can afford it.

From these numbers you'll have already guessed that if some of the small furries were too much of a strain money-wise then cats, dogs, rabbits and guinea pigs are certainly out of the question.

Different Small furries.
In general, the smaller an animal is, the shorter its lifespan. For instance, a rabbit can live up to ten years, a guinea pig around five years and you've seen the lifespan of the small furries in the last chapter. As you'll have guessed, because of the smaller cages and shorter lifespan, a mouse or hamster will be cheaper than a rat or a degu. You might just need to rejig which small furry you pick.

Fish.
Fish will be really variable depending on how many and what type you have. They have hugely different needs for things including water temperature, food and care. A couple of coldwater, freshwater fish may well be cheaper than two degus but a state-of-the-art tropical underwater heaven may not!

Chapter 9

What if You're Worried You Can't Manage Any Pet?

Above all, please believe me when I say that it is better not to get a pet at all than to neglect one. Being a responsible pet owner is all about making the right choice and sometimes that means not getting one at all. Try not to be too downhearted. Look at all your options and also think about ways things might change with time. When I was very little we had no spare money at all but as we got older my mum and dad worked hard and trained and got different jobs and as time went by we found we could get a dog. Believe me, I pestered for a LONG time before that actually happened!

If you have friends who have pets, ask if you can spend time with their animals and help them with the jobs. You never know, they might be a bit bored with it and might love to have a helper. Just being around animals is a brilliant feeling so you might need to just take small opportunities when they come along.

Talk to your mum and dad about fostering pets. There are so many unwanted pets that lots of adoption centres often need people to foster while they are waiting for a home. This might mean having rabbits, guinea pigs, small furries and even dogs and cats if you can manage, but just for a short time and often with help from the charity with the costs. You'll get some animal time but also be doing a really good deed too.

You could also find out about charities such as Hearing Dogs for Deaf People. Some of the centres ask people to care for a dog in the evenings and over the weekends while it's being trained. This means if your mum and dad are at work during the day the dog just comes to you for the times you're all at home. They have lots of different volunteering options on their website so you might find something that is perfect. A temporary arrangement might be a great compromise for you and your family.

So here we are, almost at the end of your journey into the wonderful world of small furry rodents and being an A-grade owner. All that's left to say is …

Chapter 10

WELL DONE DETECTIVES!

All together now. WELL DONE!

By the time you get to here you will have worked hard and learned exactly what it takes to be an excellent pet owner. Let's think about all the amazing things you have done and achieved since page one:

- You've learnt about how animals can make us happy and what it means to be a responsible pet owner, including the serious stuff about the law!
- You've found out that small furries are actually rodents and that it's the teeth that make a rodent a rodent.
- You've found out how the different wild small furries live, what makes them happy and what keeps them healthy.
- You've found out what food is best for small furries, which plants are safe and which are poisonous, how much food they need and how to tell if they are too fat or too thin.
- You've discovered just how much room small furries need to live happily and what sort of environment will keep them safe. SIZE MATTERS!
- You've learnt that degus, rats, mice and gerbils hate to be alone and need the company of others of the *same* species to feel safe, secure and surrounded by friends.
- You've learnt that Syrian hamsters are very different and like to be on their own. If they are mixed together they can fight and badly injure or even kill each other.
- You've found out that it's very important to let animals behave normally. Small furries need to be able to play, run, climb, dig, stretch out, chew, groom, graze, explore and, of course, eat their own poo!
- You've learnt about obesity, tooth disease, bumblefoot, wet-tail, cheek pouches and all the things you need to look out for to spot a poorly rodent before it gets too bad. You've also learnt that small furries, because they are prey animals, don't always show pain like other animals so it's up to you to know what's normal for them.
- You've done extra research, spoken to vets and nurses, been to pet shops and adoption centres, looked online, done lots of maths and maybe even made your whole family sit down together to discuss this whole pet-owning business.
- Hopefully you've even gone the whole hog and made yourself feel a bit silly wandering round the house pretending to do stuff to two or more pretend small furries.

Chapter 10

WELL DONE DETECTIVES!

THAT is a very impressive list of things and that is why you should feel very proud of yourselves. I am ecstatic that you bought or borrowed this book and read it and I am very proud of you. You may feel as if kids are ignored sometimes and you might feel sometimes like no one really listens to your opinions but I'm going to let you into a secret: you kids can change the world. Let's face it, grown-ups have messed up pet keeping for hundreds of years. They think they're too busy to do research and lots of them think they know everything already!

Just imagine if you told your mum or dad all the things you'd learned about how to actually care for small furries. I bet they would be astounded. I bet you could teach *them* some things. They might have thought it was fine to keep them in a little, glass cage! But now YOU know better. You might not feel like you can change the world but if all the children in the world learnt what you have and really took it on board then pet keeping would transform over night.

Old, wrinkly vets like me would smile and put our feet up because our workload would halve in an instant because of all those well cared for pets.

I've told you repeatedly that you should never ask yourself what sort of pet you want but now we're at the end of your journey I think it's time for you to do just that. You see, it's very important that you ask yourself what sort of animal you can care for properly but you do also need to consider what you're looking for in a pet because you and your family need to be happy too. You might have discovered that you can perfectly care for a hundred small furries but if you wanted a pet that would cuddle up on your lap every night a hundred small furries might never make you happy! Owning pets is a team game, so make sure you all talk about your options. If small furries aren't right for you have a look at the other books in the series and keep learning. All animals are fascinating, even if you don't end up with one.

If you've decided small furries would make you happy and that you can keep them happy and healthy, hang on to the book. Unless you've got a brain the size of a planet you might want to remind yourself of things when you get your new bundles of joy. When you're deciding where to get your small furries please remember adoption centres and the importance of rehoming animals.

If small furries now seem like the worst choice in the world then pass the book on. You could give it to a friend or sell it for some pocket money. If you've got a friend with a small furry that you don't think is being very well looked after you could slip the book into his or her school bag as a nudge in the right direction. If that friend gets their rat a friend or gives their gerbils a chance to dig you've taken one more step towards changing the world.

At the start of the book we said that living with animals can be wonderful. I hope the books in this series will help to guide you and your family to what will be a fantastic friendship and a time that you will look back on with big smiles and a mountain of happy memories.

© Adobe Stock

Thanks for caring about us pets.

All that remains for me to do is to tell you again how brilliant you are and to award you with your detective certificate. Proof that you now know pretty much everything there is to know about the needs of small furries.

WELL DONE!

THIS IS TO CERTIFY THAT

HAS LEARNT PRETTY MUCH **EVERYTHING**
THERE IS TO KNOW ABOUT CARING FOR SMALL FURRY RODENTS
AND BEING AN EXCELLENT PET OWNER!